Tennessee Woman

AN INFINITE VARIETY

by
Wilma Dykeman

Newport, Tennessee
Wakestone Books
1993

Library of Congress Catalog Card Number: 93-61540

Designer: Kay Jursik
Jacket illustration © the artist and may not be
reproduced in any form without permission.

For availability of our books in quantity at special discounts for
educational use, fund-raising, and other purposes,
please contact the publisher:

Wakestone Books
282 Clifton Heights Road
Newport, TN 37821
(615) 623-7394

A dedication appropriate to this book was expressed long ago by Anne Dallas Dudley, whose influence was important in ratification of the 19th amendment to the United States Constitution in the summer of 1920.

> "We have had a vision, a vision of a time when a woman's home will be the whole wide world, her children all those whose feet are bare, and her sisters all who need a helping hand; a vision of a new knighthood, a new chivalry, when men will not only fight for women but for the rights of women."

Other Books by Wilma Dykeman

THE FRENCH BROAD, A Rivers of America volume.
Holt, Rinehart & Winston.

NEITHER BLACK NOR WHITE. With James Stokely.
Holt, Rinehart & Winston.

SEEDS OF SOUTHERN CHANGE. With James Stokely.
University of Chicago Press.

THE TALL WOMAN. A novel.
Holt, Rinehart & Winston.

THE FAR FAMILY. A novel.
Holt, Rinehart & Winston.

RETURN THE INNOCENT EARTH. A novel.
Holt, Rinehart & Winston.

LOOK TO THIS DAY. Collected Essays.
Holt, Rinehart & Winston.

PROPHET OF PLENTY. University of Tennessee Press.

THE BORDER STATES. A Library of America volume. With James Stokely.
Time-Life Books.

TOO MANY PEOPLE, TOO LITTLE LOVE. *Holt, Rinehart & Winston.*

TENNESSEE: A BICENTENNIAL HISTORY.
W. W. Norton.

HIGHLAND HOMELAND: THE PEOPLE OF THE GREAT SMOKIES. With Jim
Stokely.
National Park Service volume.

THE APPALACHIAN MOUNTAINS. With Dykeman Stokely.
Text for Graphic Arts photographic study.

TENNESSEE. *Text for a Graphic Arts photographic study.*

WITH FIRE AND SWORD: THE BATTLE OF KINGS MOUNTAIN.
National Park Service.

EXPLORATIONS. A Wilma Dykeman Reader.
Wakestone Books.

In his play *Anthony and Cleopatra*
Shakespeare described one of the
most interesting women in history:

"Age cannot wither her,
nor custom stale Her infinite variety...."

Carole Bucy reversed Tennessee's historic westward migration when she moved from Texas to Nashville. Wife of a lawyer, mother of two children, community leader, she exemplifies Tennessee woman's continuing variety.

Introduction

CAROLE BUCY

I had lived in Tennessee for 14 years before I knew that our state was the 36th and deciding state to pass the suffrage amendment to the United States Constitution. I did not know that a vote in the Tennessee General Assembly in Nashville in 1920 gave women across the country the right to vote. My own grandmother, a farm woman in Texas, voted for the first time in November, 1920, after that event here in Nashville in our state's capitol. I was captivated by the story and wondered how many other stories about the accomplishments of Tennessee women had escaped notice. Although I held a Master's degree in history from a Tennessee institution, I knew very little about Tennessee's history and nothing about the women of the state other than those whose paths I had been fortunate enough to cross during my activities with the League of Women Voters.

I wanted to learn about Tennessee's history. I signed up for classes, went on tours of cemeteries, and read. When my son arrived in fourth grade, I realized that there would be a unit on Tennessee in the spring. The teachers had prepared their own materials since there were none available. This was another opportunity for me to learn more about Tennessee. While assisting

him with an assignment on the male heroes of Tennessee history
at the public library that year, I asked the librarian if there were
any books about Tennessee women. "Only the book that Wilma Dykeman did for the Decade for
Women," she replied. She then pulled the Nashville Room's worn
copy of *Tennessee Women: Past and Present* from the shelf and
handed it to me. I knew Wilma Dykeman's writing only from
reading *The Tall Woman,* the story of a woman who survived the
hardships of the Civil War and Reconstruction. I was intrigued as
I read this narrative about the toils and triumphs of Tennessee
women. Reading her text not only increased my factual knowledge about women in Tennessee, but it also planted seeds in my
mind of how often women's contributions had been overlooked
or omitted from history books. I knew none of these women, but
I was eager to make their acquaintance.

Two years later when my daughter was in fourth grade, I was
delighted to see that a textbook had now been published for
elementary teachers to use while teaching Tennessee. When she
came home with the new text, I quickly began to look for the
section on the passage of the suffrage amendment. I could not find
it. The book had a description of Sergeant Alvin York and his
action in World War I which was followed by a description of
Governor Austin Peay's accomplishments as governor in the
1920's. 1920, the year of suffrage, had not been mentioned.

At this point, I realized how much education about women's
contributions to history was needed. Over the next two years, I
discussed the problem with scholars and teachers across the state.
Everyone agreed that there was a need for materials about women
in Tennessee as well as tremendous interest on the part of classroom teachers. After all, most of Tennessee's fourth grade teachers were women and they had heard the surprising report from the

American Association of University Women about education of girls showing how the self-esteem of girls deteriorated during their years within the educational system.

I presented the problem to the League of Women Voters; the League board voted to apply for a grant from the Tennessee Humanities Council to prepare a teachers' guide and conduct a series of teacher workshops across Tennessee on incorporating women into the Tennessee social studies curriculum. When the League received the grant, I was asked to prepare the teachers' guide and conduct the workshops.

During the course of my research, I continued to go back to the Nashville Room to refer to their battered copy of *Tennessee Women: Past and Present* by Wilma Dykeman. Their copy was worn from much use and no other copies were available. Only a few thousand copies had been printed. Each time that I discovered another Tennessee woman and learned of her accomplishments, I would go back to Wilma Dykeman's text. More often than not, I could find the woman in the text, but the search required considerable time and patience.

When I began to assemble my research into the teachers' guide, I realized that every library in this state needed a copy of *Tennessee Women: Past and Present.* The text could be updated to cover the achievements of the past fifteen years with an index to assist researchers, but I became convinced that it needed to be republished.

I then presented this observation to the staff of the Humanities Council hoping that they would undertake this project. They informed me that Wilma Dykeman held the copyright for her work and suggested that I call her to describe my teachers' workshops and share with her my ideas about the republishing of her text.

When I called up Wilma Dykeman at her home in Newport, she had never met me or heard of me. She was enthusiastic about the teacher workshops. We talked for almost an hour sharing names and stories of various women in Tennessee. After several conversations about the possibilities, it was agreed that a newly revised version of her earlier *Tennessee Women* would be published.

Wilma Dykeman attended one of the League's workshops for teachers. When I introduced her, the teachers were surprised. They came up to her afterward to tell her when they had read *The Tall Woman* or *The French Broad*. They wanted her to know how much her writing had meant to them. That afternoon we sat at my kitchen table going over the text of *Tennessee Women: Past and Present* page by page. She then took the materials I had prepared for Tennessee teachers and wove many of them into her original text which she also expanded. The book that you are about to read is the result of this collaboration.

It is hoped that reading the prose of Wilma Dykeman will give the reader as much pleasure as it has given me. Women in Tennessee have accomplished much. Their stories need to be heard. When we look at our past, we need to know what the women as well as the men were doing.

With the state's bicentennial approaching every Tennessean should make an effort to learn about our state—the land, the history, the people, the infinite variety of experiences that combine to become the Tennessee experience. This is our heritage. It is who we are. Each of us, male or female, has known Tennessee woman.

Nashville, Tennessee
October 1, 1993

Tennessee Woman

AN INFINITE VARIETY

BY
WILMA DYKEMAN

I met her on a spring day many years ago.

Her weathered house nestled in a hollow surrounded by the majestic Unakas that are neighbors of the Great Smoky Mountains forming the boundary between North Carolina and Tennessee. The wrinkles in her face were etched by sun and wind and 104 years of living in harsh hill-country that yields up its bounty slowly.

"Child, I've never knowed no place but this. My mother died a-birthing me. My daddy married four times. I don't know how many brothers and sisters, halves and all, I helped to raise. And I plowed for daddy from the time I was a girl. I used a mowing blade, and an axe, and did what was needed. Daddy said he didn't know what he'd do if I got married. I said he'd just have to do like I did, make his own way."

She is Tennessee woman.

Photograph courtesy of the
Grace Moore Collection,
Frank H. McClung
Museum, University of
Tennessee, Knoxville.

GRACE MOORE

"Quite objectively I can look back on the movie, *One Night of Love*, filmed in 1934, and see what it meant in terms of music. It took grand opera to the ends of the world and brought a new public into the opera houses to rejuvenate and refresh what had become a baronial subscription art. . . . " 'It took the high-hat off opera,' editorialized the *Daily News* in New York. 'The first time in 25 years out of the red,' said the London *Times* about my Covent Garden debut after the film's great success. Here was not only personal triumph . . . It meant a new lease on life for the music I loved."
—Grace Moore in her autobiography, *You're Only Human Once.*

I met her far away from Tennessee, in the grandeur of New York's Metropolitan Opera House.

I listened as her voice rang clear and true, stirring the hearts of her audiences when she became Mimi in *La Boheme,* Tosca, Madam Butterfly, and Louise, the role for which she was coached by its great composer, Gustave Charpentier.

I discovered that **Grace Moore** was born in the lumber village of Slabtown in Tennessee's Cocke County, moved to Jellico where she sang in the church choir, and then lived in Chattanooga where her father was a successful merchant.

Beautiful, talented, and above all determined, she became a successful nightclub singer in New York—but her reach was for higher stars. She became the musical toast of American and European opera.

Grace Moore brought grace and glamour to Grand Opera, along with a measure of democracy. When she dared to break cultural barriers by singing operatic arias in popular movies, she brought a new experience of music to millions who had never been privileged to visit the few metropolitan centers of Grand Opera.

She is Tennessee woman.

I met her in the dusty pages of history, aglow with life.

"War Woman" and "Beloved Woman" she was called by her Cherokee nation. A century and a half before other American women could vote in their country's councils, **Nancy Ward** was participating in her peoples' decisive events—making war or making treaties.

When her Cherokees fought the Creeks in 1755, she lay behind a log with the warrior named Kingfisher, biting bullets to make them more deadly. When he was killed she picked up his rifle and fought until the enemy was routed. Her courage won her the honor of being a Beloved Woman, who could speak in any council and help decide the fate of prisoners. She fulfilled both roles, intervening at executions to save the lives of numerous pioneers, among them **Lydia Bean** and her son, the first white child born in Tennessee. In 1781 Nancy Ward even conducted negotiations with an invading American army; in 1785 she was one of her nation's negotiators at the first Cherokee conference with the new United States of America.

NANCY WARD

"This Woman held the office of 'Beloved Woman', which not only gave her the right
to speak in council, but conferred such great power that she might, by the wave of a
swan's wing, deliver a prisoner condemned by the council, though already tied to the
stake. She was of queenly and commanding presence and manners, and her house was
furnished in a style suitable to her high dignity. . . Like her distinguished uncle
(Attakullakulla), Nancy Ward was a consistent advocate of peace, and constant in her
good offices to both races."   —A.V. Goodpasture, *Indian Wars and Warriors*

    Cherokee attitudes toward women reflected those of their
Iroquois ancestors. The Great Law central to Iroquois culture
stated that lineal descent of their people "shall run in the female
line. Women shall be considered the progenitors of the nation.
They shall own the land and the soil. Men and women shall follow
the status of the mother."

    Vivacious and eloquent, unafraid in war but loving peace,
Nancy Ward reportedly said, when she saved Mrs. Bean from the
fire, "No woman shall be burned at the stake while I am Beloved
Woman." And when she died, "her great-grandson reported in
sworn testimony, a light rose from her body, fluttered like a bird
around the room, and finally flew out the open door."

*   She is Tennessee woman.*

I met her at lunch one day with a mutual friend. Jean Lacey and I were sharing a sandwich when she asked, "Do you know Lizzie Crozier French?" "Not really," I said. She introduced me to the wide-ranging intensity of this woman's life, which I went on to discover for myself: a woman for all seasons.

Born in 1851, only 27 years after the death of Nancy Ward, the Cherokees would certainly have considered Lizzie Crozier French a Beloved Woman, a leader in their assemblies. Her native Knoxville and Tennessee did not always accord her such praise. This did not daunt the young widow with one son who, at the age of 23, had known only two years of marriage. In 1885, she began to exert her powerful influence to win "all sorts of rights for women—educational, legal, civil, and social—rights that most women of her day were unaware they lacked."

Lizzie and two sisters began a successful school at the East Tennessee Female Institute. She believed that education could take many forms and had no limitations of age and so she organized a woman's club, the **Ossoli Circle**—Ossoli for feminist Margaret Fuller Ossoli, and Circle because men were accustomed to belonging to clubs while women belonged to church circles and masculine prerogatives would be less threatened by this familiar name for an innovative effort. Ossoli Circle, the first woman's club in Tennessee and the first federated club in the South, was part of a movement which was bringing women together, often for the first time, to share common interests, widen their intellectual horizons, and provide an opportunity for them to organize logical presentations and speak in public.

Speaking was one of Lizzie Crozier French's talents. It helped her found or lead the Woman's Education and Industrial Union, the Knoxville Pen Women, the Tennessee Federation of Women's Clubs, the Parent-Teachers' Association, the Episcopal and then the Unitarian churches, the Tennessee Equal Suffrage Association, and the League of Women Voters. It was as a "suffragist" that she listed her occupation, however.

"I wish I could say Fellow Citizens," she began one of her famous debates for woman suffrage, "but since I am not accepted as a citizen by the government, I must say Citizens and Fellow Servants."

When she suggested that Knoxville should have a police matron and no one could be found to fill the office initially, she became the first police matron in the South and held the job for several months until the city appointed a permanent matron.

When she discovered, following the suffrage victory, that no women were running for office, she became a candidate for City Council, at the age of 72. She did not win but she had broken new ground.

She fought for women to have rights to their own property, to keep the wages they earned without turning them over to their husbands, as law demanded, and to have equal guardianship of their children—to be free citizens and whole persons.

A friend wrote of Lizzie Crozier French, who "believed in the sanctity of the home, fidelity in marriage, and devotion to rearing children," that upon her death "the woman's movement has not lost her. She lives in the organizations she helped to build, in the thought she helped to direct, in the faith and purpose she inspired."

She is Tennessee woman.

I met her casually one afternoon through her photograph.

Mary Church Terrell, tall and handsome, stands in that picture with her dark upswept hair and almost-smiling countenance

MARY CHURCH TERRELL

When Mary Church Terrell was 89 years old, she led a committee that won a lawsuit ending discrimination in hotels, restaurants, buses, and other public facilities in Washington, D.C. She died the following year, having remained throughout her lifetime ahead of her region and her country in perceiving social problems and seeking their solution.

Photo courtesy of Moorland-Spingarn Research Center, Howard University, used with permission.

framed by a frilly light parasol, a Southern belle—a black Southern belle.

Born two years before the close of the Civil War, in 1863, to affluence (her father, Robert R. Church, born in legal bondage was an early black financier and political leader in Memphis), educated at Oberlin College, she married a Harvard graduate who was appointed by President Theodore Roosevelt to the first federal judgeship held by an African American.

This attractive woman could have lived a life of personal pleasure and indulgence. Instead, she became a teacher to her people, and then a civic leader speaking and organizing against racial injustice, especially that suffered by black women. When she was the first president of the Colored Women's League of Washington and then the first president of the National Association of Colored Women, she advocated day care centers, nursing schools, and special work with sharecroppers.

When Mary Church Terrell focused attention on the plight of sharecroppers, she was addressing the situation of unknown numbers of women whose labor in southern fields was essential to the survival of their families.

During the decades after the Civil War and into the twentieth century across much of the rural south a legal bondage was replaced by economic bondage, this one shackling both blacks and whites.

In the system called sharecropping a landowner provided a house, a share of the crop—usually cotton—and sometimes garden space in exchange for a year's farm work by a man and his family. The field work of his wife and children became his main asset. If the sharecropper had to help buy seed, which was usually in the contract, and perhaps feed for mules and horses while he went into debt to the landowner for his family's food, medicine and clothing, the family often found itself sinking each year into a deeper quagmire of debt.

Hardship fell in unequal burden on the woman. Childbearing, care-giving, household chores were singularly her own even as she joined in the toil of planting, cultivating, and harvesting the crops that ruled her own and her family's life.

They were voiceless in their own time and they are nameless in the pages of history, these women who knew little youth, scant joy, and no security throughout their harsh existence. Mary Church Terrell's concern did not reform or abolish sharecropping. It would also be several decades before day care centers and nursery schools she advocated were seriously and widely considered. But like many others ahead of their time in speaking for "the least of these" she raised one voice in a vast silence.

In 1895 she became the first black woman appointed to the District of Columbia Board of Education. During World War I she fought for equality for black soldiers. She wrote ("What It Means to Be Colored In the Capital of the United States"), picketed (major business firms that were unjust in their practices), and was called "the mother of the sit-in." Friend of the famous and the unknown, honored by universities and national and international organizations, Mary Church Terrell bequeathed important advice to her fellow Americans: "Keep on going, keep on insisting, keep on fighting injustice."

She is Tennessee woman.

I met her reluctantly, by appointment, because I needed to know some facts of Tennessee history and political life that only she could tell me. I discovered a trailblazer who had been ahead of her state, her region, her country, her sex, her race, and many of her friends on such a wide range of issues that simply to list them looked like an agenda for democracy at work, democracy to be achieved in the 20th-century. She had been chairman of the board of the Chattanooga Public Library, vice-chairman of the Tennessee Commission on Children, Democratic National Committeewoman, president of the Tennessee Council on Human Relations, chairman of the state advisory committee to the U.S. Commission on Civil Rights, and catalyst-founder-leader in women's organizations as a truly pioneer feminist.

Martha Ragland, wife of a successful businessman, mother of a son and daughter, with entree coveted by many to elite social circles, chose in the 1930's during her early thirties, to make her circle of life inclusive rather than exclusive. With intelligence, skill and determination she entered the public arena.

Newspaper reporters described her in different ways: "The

slim, five-feet-three-and-a-half inches Chattanooga homemaker and political leader. . ." or "Mrs. Ragland has one of those delightful spoon bread-and-honey accents and is just as feminine as the traditional moonlight and magnolia belle of the old South. But something new has been added and that's the discovery that politics is a fascinating game which can be learned by women, played by women, and used to make homes and communities happier, healthier and free of gang or boss rule."

Free! That was the key word. She could be traditional and winning—telling male political workers, "A woman can't be effective in her political work without the approval of her family"—and she could be candid and compelling—writing a famous Southern editor who derided a woman candidate for President, "I believe we need more women who are willing to assume serious responsibilities. . . . It would help if you would report their efforts factually without the tongue-in-cheek and knife-in-back overtones." But always the purpose was to secure more freedom for someone to whom it was denied.

When she helped organize Planned Parenthood groups in Knoxville and Chattanooga and at the state level in the 1930's and early 1940's, and when she worked to get birth control clinics in public health in Tennessee, she was moved by a realization of how many unwanted children were born to despairing, uninformed parents each year. They needed freedom to choose their family's size, freedom to save mothers' lives; eventually it would be recognized as freedom to help solve the most explosive of the world's problems-too many people on too small a planet.

In 1938 Martha Ragland invited **Margaret Sanger** to come to Tennessee; as they visited the four major cities, crowds double the size expected came to hear the internationally acclaimed leader.

In Nashville, the state commissioner of institutions and welfare introduced Mrs. Sanger: "I present to you a woman who is a pioneer, a patriot, and a realist." He might also have been describing Martha Ragland. If she had not been a realist before, her entrance into politics would have made her one. Initiation came through the League of Women Voters: she was president of the Chattanooga League, and of the state organization, and then served on the national board. An editorial in *The Chattanooga Times* summarized some of her interests: "One of the first campaigns was that forcing proper milk standards here. While constantly striving for better health services, better housing and general social improvement, for the juvenile court, for tax equalization, etc. Mrs. Ragland has been a mighty factor in arousing the electorate to its responsibility at the polls." Publication in 1946 of *Tennessee Needs A New Constitution* was part of her effort at basic reform.

In 1948 Martha Ragland launched the activity that would reveal her distinctive genius. She organized a statewide women's division of the Estes Kefauver-for-Senator campaign. It was the first of five such state-wide campaigns she would lead, almost always with success. Her master's degree in political science from Vanderbilt hadn't exactly prepared this woman for the in-fighting that characterized Tennessee politics and activities of the Democratic party at the national level, but she was no less astute at learning in this school than in more formal classrooms. And the battles she fought were most often concerned with openness: freeing voters from the poll tax, opening political leadership to blacks and women, freeing party control from "vested interests" and "a few superannuated professional politicians," freeing women from an ancient sense of inferiority that inhibits their full influence in the life of their home or their planet—discovering and divulging the ways in which those inhibitions are consciously or unconsciously strengthened.

When Martha Ragland assumed her initial task of political organization for her candidate, Estes Kefauver, a letter was sent to women across the state. It began: "Here it is spring again, and the jonquils are in bloom, and no one seems to be thinking much about politics. But I have two children and am very much interested in the worsening world situation. . . ." Martha Ragland, able to see both the jonquils in her garden and the destructive forces threatening human freedom anywhere, everywhere, wrote that.

An effective political force herself, Democratic National Vice-Chairman India Edwards once said that Martha Ragland was the most capable political organizer, male or female, she had known. In Tennessee and in the nation, Martha Ragland always knew that politics was and is too important to be left to the politicians.

She is Tennessee woman.

These are only a few, an inspiring symbolic few, of that great throng past and present that compose the still unfinished portrait of Tennessee Woman. Some of them, all too few of them, are included in this brief book. Readers can share with the writer a growing awareness that any exploration of Tennessee women's lives is surrounded by contradictory sensations of frustration and fulfillment. Frustration arises because there is so little solid material or evaluation of women included in otherwise definitive histories and reference works illuminating the state's past and present. Fulfillment flows from the realization that there is so much to discover and understand about the private and public lives and contributions and unrealized potential of one major segment of our population.

Recognizing that this survey can neither make amends for all past omissions nor call attention to all the plain and subtle challenges yet to be met, its purpose becomes two-fold: to inform and inspire. The information reaches out to embrace a wide range of lives, talents, beauty and brutality, wasted efforts, unrealized dreams, and amazing achievements. From them comes the inspiration. It is the inspiration to search out and discover others unknown or little-known who can reveal so much about our place, our past, ourselves.

In one sense, then, many of those who read this book must continue writing it. In their own search of the past, through mothers and grandmothers and friends and old familiar documents or oral accounts, or through more formal channels of historical research, they can stimulate new awareness of the present and expand horizons for the future.

Those from the past are out there awaiting our discovery of them. We meet their names in many places: the **Granny White** Pike, the **Nancy Ross** sweet potato, a minor planet named **Rhoda**, an international sanctuary for worship at the United Nations designated the **Sadie Wilson Tillman** chapel—the variety of their contributions seems endless.

And never forget the nameless, silent, forgotten ones—those whose sweat has poured down in fields and factories, whose blood has ebbed away on home battlefields and in hospitals, whose tears have spilled down cheeks red and black and white and brown, whose laughter has lightened heavy moments, whose faith has withstood betrayal, whose hope has out-distanced cynicism, whose ideals have proved over the long reach of time to be the sturdiest foundations of reality.

Their homes have been mansions—Nashville's Belmont, built by thrice-married **Adelicia Hayes Franklin Acklen Cheatham**, who lived from 1817 to 1887, reputedly the nation's wealthiest woman for at least a decade. Well-educated (as a child she learned five languages), she proved resourceful in managing the six Louisiana cotton plantations she inherited from her first husband, Isaac Franklin. With her equally shrewd second husband she continued to live at their handsome estate, Belmont. During the Civil War, after Joseph Acklen's death while in Mississippi trying to sell their cotton crop, she managed to persuade a Confederate general and a daring ship's captain to release her cotton crop from the Confederacy and run the Union blockade. In England Adelicia Acklen's cotton sold for $900,000 in gold.

She was successful in finances and war but not in her third marriage. She moved to New York, leaving her Belmont mansion with its gardens, zoo, aviary, and one unique asset: running water throughout the house at a time before even the White House in Washington enjoyed such luxury.

Their homes have been small farms scattered along dirt roads lacing the flat lands and woods to the west, the rolling hill country and bluegrass fields of the mid-state, or the steep mountains and hidden valleys of the east.

On such a farm **Mary Cameron** was born in Grainger County where she lived until her father died when she was fifteen. Her mother had died when Mary was only four years old. Leaving the farm, as so many were forced to do over the generations as they sought a livelihood, Mary faced a new frontier when she went to work in a garment factory in Knoxville. There she became a leader in the early 1940's in the International Ladies' Garment Workers' Union. She sought better working and living standards for women in industry.

Sometimes their homes have not found early roots. For young **Oprah Winfrey**, as for many children whose parents did not know a settled married life, "home" was a series of adjustments to different places, different people. One of the places she called "home," in that time before she was welcomed around the world, was Nashville, Tennessee.

Until she was six years old Oprah lived in Mississippi with her grandmother. Then she moved to Nashville where she spent the next three years with her father. From the age of nine to fourteen Oprah lived with her mother in a Milwaukee ghetto, and then the teenager returned to Nashville to live with her father.

She liked to act and would sometimes give readings from the powerful speeches of Sojourner Truth, the great woman who had led so many of her people out of bondage along the freedom road north before the Civil War.

When Oprah was 17 and a student at Nashville's East High School, she had a job at a local radio station, WVOL. Three years later she was working her way through Tennessee State University but she did not graduate. She had found a place in television at WTVF, Nashville's Channel 5. The rest is history. She worked in Baltimore and in Chicago, in movies, and eventually as mistress of her own talk show.

But in 1987 Oprah returned to Nashville to complete her senior project and receive her degree from TSU. This fulfilled a promise she had made to her father, Vernon Winfrey, a Nashville barber and Metro Councilman. In September, 1993, Oprah Winfrey

OPRAH WINFREY

Oprah Winfrey experienced early and intimately many of the "problems" crying for attention in our society today. Her triumph over those experiences is legendary. Sixteen Emmy Awards for the television talk-show watched by some 20 million viewers daily, plus a substantial personal fortune, is tangible evidence of her success. Discussing her forthcoming biography at a meeting of the American Booksellers Association, she announced she was going to bring people into bookstores who had never been there before. Her book was going to change their lives. As had *Roots*, she might have added, the book written by her friend, Alex Haley, whose farm she visited not long before his death.
Photo courtesy WSMV Channel 4, Nashville.

was Number One on the list of highest paid members of the nation's entertainment industry. She had found a home in millions of homes.

Tennessee women have nurtured tradition, building churches and clubs and schools, and preserving historical sites and treasures.

And they have broken tradition, as did **Lillie Ladd Mauser**, grandmother of former U. S. Senator Howard Baker.

In April, 1927, Lillie Ladd accompanied her husband, the Roane County Sheriff, to Mayo Hospital for treatment of a serious illness. While they were away, 12 prisoners escaped from the Kingston jail. Mrs. Ladd took the first train back to Tennessee and enlisted the only prisoner left in the jail to chauffeur her into the hills. When two of the escaped prisoners were sighted and approached, the "woman sheriff pro-tem" persuaded them to accompany her back to the county jail to finish their sentences. A local newspaper reported that one of the escapees said that Mrs. Ladd had been "awfully good to him while he was in prison and although he would not surrender to any man or any other woman, he would become her prisoner and return." On the way back to jail, the party stopped at the home of the second escapee and enjoyed "a real country dinner."

In a statement about the episode, Acting Sheriff Lillie Ladd indicated that "pistols, shotguns, highpowered rifles and the like are obsolete equipment to her; she can get better results by rapid-fire conversation and getting the confidence of the wanted men." She was confident she would have all the escapees back behind bars in a reasonable length of time.

When her husband died, Mrs. Ladd served as sheriff for an interval, following the trail blazed shortly before by **Laura Mason** of Wilson County, who finished her husband's term as sheriff when he died in 1928, and then won election on her own to fill that office, the first woman in the nation to be elected sheriff.

And why not?

Why?

These are the questions women have asked again and again in quiet moments, in crucial times, to arouse thought, stimulate action, make a difference.

"Ask why!" Scotswoman **Frances Wright,** who tried to found in Tennessee a Utopia based on absolute equality, preached to enraptured audiences.

"Why can't we have a national park in the Great Smokies?" **Annie May Davis** asked her husband in Knoxville in the summer of 1923, after they had made a trip through western national parks. And an idea and movement that had been stirring many minds began to take definite shape.

"Why?" **Lizzie Crozier French** asked a young housewife in

Nashville who was escorting her to make a speech to Tennessee legislators early in the century, "why do you not want to vote?" And the young housewife decided she did want to vote.

Ruth Webb O'Dell, "Lady Ruth," who had given, at her death in 1956, forty-one years in public service and education, and was one of the first women to be elected to the Tennessee legislature, asked why young people who were getting married should not have to pass a medical examination to safeguard their own health and that of society. It was an important health provision for all Tennesseans.

She also asked why Cocke County history should not be preserved, and in a veritable storehouse of a volume, *Over the Misty Blue Hills*, now a collector's item for local history students, she published material that resulted from decades of dedicated search and collection. Many of her sister historians around the state have contributed town and county and family chronicles that connect us with the past in intimate, interesting details.

"Why can't . . ."

"Why shouldn't . . ."

"Why not . . ."

"Why?"

In these pages meet some of the women who have asked, and their multitude of answers. They are Tennessee woman.

Chroniclers of the time say only that it was "early in the year," but we might suppose it to be at the first opening of spring, when

CHARLOTTE ROBERTSON

Charlotte Robertson was at her husband's side in establishing the Watauga settlement in East Tennessee and Fort Nashboro on the Cumberland River in Middle Tennessee. Like other pioneer women, she labored in the fields as well as in the cabin, tended livestock as well as children. Perhaps more than any other Tennessee woman, she helped repel Indian attacks on white settlers. On a flatboat going down the Tennessee, she wielded an oar against warriors fighting for the land they believed to be theirs. Later, in Fort Nashboro, she loosed dogs and routed attackers. With all the challenges she met, Charlotte seems to have had no problems with stress or tension. She died at age 92, in 1843. Photo courtesy of the Tennessee State Museum.

mountain trails were soggy underfoot and the pungent smell from deep layers of decaying leaves filled the chilly morning air, when mountain rivers were swollen with melting snow and delicate trailing arbutus flowered in crannied ledges. In early spring of 1770 two explorer-settlers swung down from the mountains into an opening in what was then the northwesternmost part of North Carolina, an area that would eventually be part of the state of Tennessee. That clearing was called the Watauga Old Fields.

The man who was an adventurer first and settler second was named Daniel Boone, and the settler who had turned temporary adventurer was James Robertson. Robertson looked this new land over well and then returned to Wake County, North Carolina, where he had lived for the past 13 years, since leaving his home in Virginia at the age of 15. Back in the Piedmont he collected his wife, Charlotte, one child, and some ten other families and set into motion a removal to the Western Waters, as the land beyond the Blue Ridge was called.

James Robertson's reaction to the new country "out yonder" was typical. The first move he made was to go back and get his wife and children and bring them with him to make a home. It was, indeed, presence of women on the frontier which, from the first, set settlements of men from the British Isles apart from most of those of Spain or France. Men of any nationality might bring their guns or Bibles to conquer a wilderness land and its people, but when they brought their wives, too, some quality of solidity and permanence was added that could change the course of history.

From the beginning of white settlement in Tennessee, the primary and paramount role of women in private and public life was as wife and mother. Of the more than 700 listings in the index of the fifth-to-seventh grade state history that has been described as "the most widely adopted of history textbooks" over a 25-year period, seven refer to specific women. Five of these are mentioned only because of their husbands: John Sevier "married **Miss Catherine Sherrill**, who has been called his 'Bonnie Kate.'" During an Indian attack in 1781, on Fort Nashborough, "**Mrs. Robertson**, it is said, turned out of the fort about fifty fierce dogs and set them on the Indians." A dual entry for Sam Houston tells of his marriage to **Miss Eliza Allen**, a union which lasted from January to April of 1829, and later marriage to **Miss Margaret Lea** from Alabama, by whom "he reared in Texas a family of two sons and four daughters." When troublesome bonded indebtedness of the state was settled in 1883, among the bonds settled at full value were some "belonging to **Mrs. Polk**, the widow of President James K. Polk." The other two entries concern the Beloved Woman of the Cherokees, **Nancy Ward**, and Governor William Blount's daughter, **Barbara**, who attended classes at

Blount College (later the University of Tennessee) and became America's first coed.

A stranger from outer space reading such textbooks would have little notion that approximately half the population of Tennessee has been female. Students learning from such texts might also infer that the "important" work was carried forth almost exclusively by men. Occasional flowery references to helpmeets and motherhood may have sweetened political orations or funeral eulogies, but they could scarcely overcome daily evidence pervading every aspect of life that these roles were considered minor and taken for granted. Little wonder that Attakullakulla, Little Carpenter, Cherokee chief from the Overhill towns in the Tennessee country, was shocked when he went to an early council with whites and found no women present. He asked whether it was not true that "White men as well as the Red were born of Women." Generations later he might have been asking the same question.

It has not been the thrust of women for equal rights and honor that humbles their central experience of home creation, wifehood, motherhood. Any sense of ignominy surrounding that experience surely grows from economic deprivation and intellectual and cultural neglect.

Anyone who makes acquaintance with some of the women in this account must admit that certain qualities are common to almost all of them. (Never let it be said that any generalization could include all Tennessee women; they refuse such conformity.) Two dominant characteristics are their courage and variety. Certainly these qualities are not unique to any group of people, but courage and variety of a special kind can be discovered in representative women.

The courage has been physical: that of John Donelson's voyagers from the Long Island of the Holston in East Tennessee to the French Salt Springs (Nashville) on the Cumberland, in winter of 1779-80, when **Mrs. Jennings, Mrs. Peyton,** and a nameless "Negro woman" rescued the Jennings' boat from capture by Indians. They waded into the water to loose the boat from rocks where it had lodged. Donelson recorded in his diary that Mrs. Peyton had been "delivered of an infant" the night before she helped in the rescue, "exposed to wet and cold." Following their "wonderful escape" it was discovered that the baby had been killed "in the hurry and confusion," and that even the women's clothes "were very much cut with bullets, especially Mrs. Jennings's."

The courage has been social and political: that of **Mary Morrison,** when she protested against the passage of Jim Crow laws and on a July day in 1905 in Memphis refused to accept a back seat in the segregated public streetcar. Although she lost her case in the courts she won self-respect and became part of an early little-known Jim Crow protest that reached across the state. Five years before, at the turn of the century, **Mrs. A. Watkins;** had stated the reasonable request of all black persons: "We only want our rights as law-abiding citizens."

The courage has been of the mind and spirit: that of Knoxville's **Patricia Neal** and **Jane Merchant.** The first, an award-winning actress of acclaimed talent and intelligence, gave the world her most inspired performance when she overcame a severe stroke to return to stage and movies in full possession of her faculties and powers. Her leadership has helped countless others suffering crippling illness turn the millstone of their affliction into a stepping stone of achievement.

Jane Merchant was a bedfast poet, crippled and confined,

who eventually lost even her precious eyesight and hard-won ability to use a typewriter—while she continued to create sparkling verse wrought from everyday experiences with bright wit and deep faith, for a national as well as local audience.

As the state is varied in its geography, in its natural resources, and in many other ways, so its women are varied. Their variety and versatility go hand in hand, from earliest days to the present. Four times as long as it is wide, Tennessee stretches from the forested pinnacles of the Great Smokies and the Unakas on its eastern border to the wide fertile plains of the mighty Mississippi in the west. And its women have sung the lonely highland ballads which were part of the Scotch-Irish and English heritage, and the lonesome blues which grew out of the river-and-cotton culture and African-American roots. Except for Missouri, Tennessee exceeds any other state in the number of states on its borders. Influences spill over, and the Tennessee woman may have something of the middle Kentucky bluegrass belle, the eastern Kentucky or southwestern Virginia or western North Carolina mountaineer, the Georgia or Alabama or Mississippi lowlander, or the westering Arkansas and Missouri neighbor in her own character and lifestyle.

Here are:

The women who made the necessities of life into works of art. Cherokee and earlier Chickasaw, Creek, and Yuchi, who took honeysuckle vines, cane from the river banks, and strips of white oak from the woods and wove useful, handsome baskets. Those later settlers who created distinctive beauty in the coverlets and quilts to keep their families warm; and in the fibers they spun and dyed and wove into clothes and household goods; and in the cornshuck dolls and other play-pretties to entertain their children. When **Marian Heard** organized the first Craftsman's Fair at Gatlinburg and planned the nationally acclaimed Arrowmont School, she was among the first to recognize and preserve the creativity of many nameless women.

And those women in the "fine arts" who have often remained a minority and also unknown. Statues and ornamental works by sculptor, **Belle Kinney,** born in 1890, beautify her native Nashville as well as Chattanooga, Annapolis, New York and our nation's capital. Paintings by Knoxville's **Catherine Wiley** are in the Metropolitan Museum of Art in New York. To be sure that these and other Tennessee women will be fully represented in the National Museum of Women in the Arts in Washington, D. C. **"Perk" Prater** of Morristown, herself an artist, has led in making the state and the museum acquainted with each other.

Here, too, are:

The women who could find all they sought in a world bounded by four walls, such a one as McMinnville's **Virginia French,** writing in the late 1850's:

> The empire I would have in one sweet home
> With two hearts dwelling in it: I'd not seek
> To sway but one, for that is all the world!

And here are the women who strained against all boundaries, such a one as daring **Phoebe Fairgrave Omlie,** soaring away from earth into the high clear freedom of the sky, teaming up with her husband, Vernon, to bring general aerial service and stunt flying and aerial photography to Memphis in the rickety aircraft of the 1920's.

By 1940, **Cornelia Fort,** born in Nashville in 1919, had re-

CORNELIA FORT

"I loved it [flying] best because it taught me
utter self-sufficiency, the ability to remove
oneself beyond the keep of anyone at all
and, in so doing, it taught me what was of
value and what was not. . . If I die
violently, who can say it was 'before my
time?' I should have dearly loved to have a
husband and children. My talents in that
line would have been pretty good, but if
that is not to be, I want no one to grieve
me."   —Cornelia Fort in a 1942
                                        letter to her mother.

Photo courtesy of Dudley Fort

ceived her licenses for private and commercial flying and joined
President Franklin D. Roosevelt's Civilian Pilot's Training Program. On December 7, 1941, she witnessed the Japanese attack
on Pearl Harbor. Two years later she became the first female
American pilot to be killed while on active military duty. She was
23 years old.

How pleased Phoebe Omlie and Cornelia Fort would have
been to cry "Bon Voyage" in 1985 to petite, blonde **Dr. Rhea
Seddon**, of Murfreesboro. A woman astronaut, she broke the
"surly bonds of earth" into far reaches of space.

Here are women who defied more subtle, often crueler, bonds
of human making, such a one as **Gwen Harold Terasaki**, a young
Johnson City girl who married a Japanese diplomat and was
deported, with her young daughter, **Mariko**, to Japan during
World War II. From that harsh experience she wrote a book,
Bridge to the Sun, to increase understanding between East and

West. As a best-selling book and a movie it bequeathed a challenge to her daughter and grandchildren and all generations.

Here are:

The women who began life as Tennesseans and found fame elsewhere, such a one as lively **Hattie Caraway**, born in Bakerville, who was living in Arkansas when she became the first woman elected to the United States Senate. Or **Jean Faircloth** of Murfreesboro, who made a trip to the Orient in 1937 and met General Douglas MacArthur, whom she married. Following World War II she was given a number of medals and citations for "outstanding and unselfish courage" for remaining on Corregidor and other dangerous battlefields "when she could have run away." Or astute and charming **Polly Bergen**, whose acting and business enterprises took her from East Tennessee around the world.

And here are the women who became Tennesseans, adopting it for better or worse as their home, such a one as **Ann Phillips Rodgers Grundy**, who came to Nashville with her lawyer husband, Felix Grundy, from Kentucky, and in 1820 gave birth to her twelfth child, welcomed her first grandchild, and founded a non-denominational Union Sunday School (a full year for any woman!). The school's basic effort was to teach reading to children too poor to attend school or church. Criticized at first as "a scheme of the devil," a Sunday School became a part of every church in Nashville within three years.

Or, here is poised and wealthy **Anna Russell Cole**, born in Georgia in 1846, whose many philanthropies centered upon the educational, cultural and civic life of Nashville, where she spent her married life influencing through traditional channels by traditional means a wide spectrum of people.

Or **May Cravath Wharton,** born in Minnesota, who arrived in Pleasant Hill in 1917 and eventually brought a dream of better rural health to fruition, gaining the affectionate title "Doctor Woman of the Cumberlands."

Or indefatigable **Christine Noble Govan,** who came to Chattanooga from New York and entertained generations of young 20th-century readers with tales of their Tennessee past and stories from her lively imagination - while she was also wife, mother, and mother-in-law to a lively family of productive Tennessee authors.

Here are:

The fighters, such a woman as **Antoinette Barker,** who fought for her husband's life. At the decisive Battle of King's Mountain in South Carolina in October, 1780, Thomas Barker was one of the Tories defeated and captured by the victorious Patriots, many of them Over-Mountain men from the Tennessee country. Thomas Barker was saved from hanging by the intervention of his Washington and Sullivan County neighbors, but he was imprisoned at Jonesboro and after a year and ten months was brought to trial. Before a court that had already ordered three horse thieves to the gallows, several Tories to prison, and some offenders to the public whipping-posts, Antoinette Barker stood to appeal for a trial by jury for her husband. One historian recorded that "she did not weep, go into hysterics, faint, fall down and be carried out, but she stood up in the presence of that court, in all the magnificence of superior womanhood, and, with the vehement eloquence of despair, pleaded the cause of her husband," using the Declaration of Independence and the destitute condition of her children to support her plea. She won her case.

Here is **Nancy Cox** of Jackson County. When food became so scarce during the Civil War that women made "coffee" from

MARY JONES

"Mother Jones" she was called by
those for whom she was friend and
advocate. She spoke her purpose and
tactics plainly:
"I reside where there is a good fight."
"Fight like hell till you go to heaven."
"I don't believe in women's rights nor
in men's rights. I believe in human
rights."

Photo used with permission.

parched rye and from okra and persimmon seeds, salt could no
longer be found for curing such meat as was available. Nancy
drove a yoke of oxen into Kentucky, braving both Confederate
and Union sympathizers and, worst of all, the ruthless bushwhackers who stole from everyone. With her plodding oxen she brought
home a welcome supply of salt.

And here is Mary Harris, born in Ireland in 1830, who came
to teach in Memphis where she married George Jones, a black-
smith and organizer for the Iron Moulder's Union. They lived
near the foundry where George worked, and Mary traveled with
him on some of his "missionary work" for "the first successful
union to organize members across state lines." Within four years
they had four children. Then, in 1867, an epidemic of yellow fever
struck Memphis.

Later, in her autobiography, **Mary Jones** wrote of those tragic
days: "The victims were mainly among the poor and the workers.
The rich and the well-to-do fled the city. Schools and churches

were closed. . . The poor could not afford nurses. . . . The dead surrounded us. They were buried at night quickly and without ceremony. All about my house I could hear weeping and the cries of delirium. One by one, my four little children sickened and died. I washed their little bodies and got them ready for burial. My husband caught the fever and died. I sat alone through nights of grief. . . . After the union had buried my husband, I got a permit to nurse the sufferers. This I did until the plague was stamped out."

From Memphis, Mary Jones went to Chicago and into the dressmaking business, which was wiped out in the great fire of 1871. From that moment on she did not "try to accumulate any possessions or make a home for herself. 'I reside wherever there is a good fight against wrong,' she used to say." As a crusader for the rights of labor, especially in the nation's mines, this tiny woman (five feet tall), sedately dressed (often in black silk with a lace jabot at her throat), "blue-eyed, pink-skinned, white-haired," became known as Mother Jones. Her tongue could plead like an angel's or swear like a demon's, and a contemporary reporter called her "the greatest fighting spirit that American womanhood has developed in our time."

More recently, here is **Septima Clark,** who had taught in the South Carolina school system since 1916 until she lost her job in 1956 when she admitted affiliation with the National Association for the Advancement of Colored People. She began a fight for her pension rights, a struggle which was to take 20 years before the state would place her in the permanent appropriations file, and at Highlander Folk School in Tennessee she continued teaching, through workshops and through writing, the basics of citizenship. The National Education Association awarded Septima Clark its highest race relations honor. Other organizations and institutions recognized the sustained indignation and dignity with which this woman sought to abolish all second-class citizenship. When Martin Luther King, Jr. was presented the Nobel Peace Prize she was one of the Americans present for the ceremony. Tennessee had become her second home but the world was her classroom.

Here is **Floreine Rankin Alexander** who saw a need in her community of Maryville. Her husband was principal of an elementary school until the birth of his son and namesake, Andrew Lamar, when he went to work at an aluminum plant for twice his principal's salary. For some 25 years he served on the school board and education continued to be a frequent topic of dinner table talk. When pre-schools and kindergartens were still uncommon, Flo Alexander saw a need and pioneered in early-childhood education. Early in the 1940's, she opened a private nursery school and kindergarten in a wooden garage in the back yard. Twenty years later she helped persuade the local school board to support public kindergartens. Little wonder that Flo Alexander's son carried her appetite for innovation into his role as Tennessee's Governor, the University of Tennessee's President, and the United States' Secretary of Education.

Here are:

Women who were the nation's First Ladies—**Rachel Donelson Jackson, Sarah Childress Polk, Eliza McCardle Johnson**—illustrating in their own characters the courage and versatility which could contribute to the achievement of three significant Presidents.

Such a one was Rachel, and who does not know the story of the girl who came to Nashville on her father's, John Donelson's, flatboat during that historic river voyage, married Lewis Robards of Kentucky from whom she soon separated, and then remarried,

RACHEL DONELSON JACKSON

In a place and time where large families were customary, Rachel and Andrew Jackson had no children. They adopted four of her nephews and Andrew brought home from his war against the Creeks a little boy named Linkoya who became a part of their household.

Victim of one of the fiercest political campaigns in American history, Rachel died after her husband's election as President of the United States but before he was sworn into office. She never became first lady of her country, only of her devoted husband who, like an eagle, mated once and for life. Used with permission.

this time a young Nashville lawyer boarding at her mother's house, before her divorce from Robards was legal. Rachel and Andrew Jackson spent the rest of their lives paying penalty for that legal technicality; remarried, their devotion to each other became legendary. Such were the rigid mores and political brutalities of the time, however, that, as biographer Gerald W. Johnson has said, "the record scarred for life a perfectly innocent woman and a man guilty of nothing worse than ignorance of Virginia procedure," the state where Robards had sued for divorce. Finally, the gossip, the snide attacks weakened Rachel's resolve. She did not live to occupy the White House, to become the First Lady to the nation as she had always been to the man elected President only six weeks before her death. "Poor Rachel was spared nothing," Johnson continues, "Born to hardship, danger and toil; bound to heavy, exacting labor all her life. . . the wife of a fighting man who was twice brought home to her half dead, and whom she had to send to war three times; caught at last in the collision of political forces far beyond her comprehension, much less her control. . . ." She was "industrious, merry-hearted, loyal and kind," and her husband "did not merely value her and respect her. He loved her, as well. In addition to the long list of her recognizable merits, Rachel had the intangible, indescribable thing called personality. Her husband adored her. . . . He could, and for thirty-five long years he did, treat her with a courtesy, consideration and thoughtfulness in which no amount of breeding could have perfected him.

"Moderns are inclined to smile at the scene, often described, of Andrew Jackson sitting on one side of the hearth and his wife on the other, each puffing a long-stemmed clay pipe. But happiness and content are in the picture." In Rachel, Andrew Jackson found "the greatest good fortune of his life, a woman capable of inspiring Benton's fine line: 'Her greatest eulogy is in the affection which he bore her living, and in the sorrow with which he mourned her dead.' "

Rachel was an inspirer; Sarah was an inspirer and an adviser.

Sarah Childress met James K. Polk: when he was attending a boys' school in her home town of Murfreesboro. After they were married the young lawyer discussed his first cases with his wife and she helped him formulate his pleas. As he moved into the Tennessee legislature and then to the U.S. Congress for seven consecutive terms, and into the governor's office, and finally to the Presidency of the United States, he continued to seek Sarah's advice on issues of the day and her assistance in writing speeches. She was a poised, literate, intelligent First Lady who frustrated certain elements of Washington society when she adhered to strict

SARAH CHILDRESS POLK

No dancing in the White House?
No alcoholic beverages served at the
White House functions?
Washington was shocked. But Sarah
Polk, like many Tennessee women, lived
up to her own expectations of herself
first—and second to the expectations of
social arbiters.

Her husband had promised that, if
elected, he would serve only one term.
At the end of those four years, he and
Sarah returned to Tennessee. Within a
year he died of Cholera. Sarah died in
1891 at age 88, esteemed by all who
knew of her contribution to her state
and her country.
Used with permission.

rules of sobriety and propriety. Her dauntless character won their respect.

Respect, too, was the homage paid Andrew Johnson's wife and daughter. It was the latter, **Martha**, wife of Tennessee Senator David Patterson, acting as First Lady for her father when her mother was ill, who told a newspaper reporter when she first went to the White House: "We are a plain people, sir, from the mountains of Tennessee, and we do not propose to put on airs because we have the fortune to occupy this place for a little while."

Eliza McCardle met Andrew Johnson on an autumn afternoon in 1826 when the black-haired young former apprentice was moving to the village of Greeneville to support himself and his mother at the tailor's trade. The following May they were married and 18-year-old Eliza started preparing her husband for the career that would carry him to the Presidency of the United States.

ELIZA McCARDLE JOHNSON

The daughter of a shoemaker who had
come to Tennessee from Scotland, Eliza
McCardle knew the value of literacy. Few
of the many Tennessee women who have
struggled to open to family or students
the world of reading and the power of the
written word have achieved Eliza's success. Her husband's summit of success as
President of the United States was not to
be fully enjoyed, however. Her own fragile health and the turmoil of his public life
overshadowed strong support of Tennessee's public school system, still in its
weak infancy, and establishment of a state
library and archives. The influence of a
wife who encouraged a young tailor to
read and write reaches into today.
Used with permission.

Andrew could spell and read. She taught him, patiently and
laboriously, to write and to do sums in arithmetic. As he worked
at his tailor's bench, she read aloud to him. He particularly liked
the articles about politics, and they collected clippings of speeches;
Andrew began to practice making speeches, while Eliza listened
and made suggestions.

Historian **Kathleen Prindiville** has described the role—the
several roles—Eliza Johnson played in her husband's career:
"Their daughter Martha was born the year he was elected to his
first public office, that of a Greeneville alderman, but Eliza still
found time to study with him. As he advanced into state and
national politics she took up a new work. The pupil no longer
needed a teacher, but he did need someone to care for his private
business while he devoted himself to public office; so Eliza became
the business manager of the household. While he served in the
state legislature and in Congress, she stayed at Greeneville, school-

ing her family, collecting rents, and directing improvements on the land and buildings which they had thriftily bought. She was there in the little mountain town when President Lincoln appointed Andrew, then United States Senator, to be Military Governor of Tennessee."

Her versatility was matched by her courage as the Confederates confiscated her home and she made her way through hostile territory to join her Governor husband, and later as she sat in the White House, ill and helpless, throughout the long days of his impeachment trial. Her husband's acquittal and subsequent return to the U.S. Senate vindicated, at least in large measure, the plodding effort, the boundless faith that Eliza Johnson had poured into their marriage and his career.

Here, with the inspirers, are also the inspired, using many talents and tools to reveal their inspiration.

The bench and bar provided **Camille McGee Kelley** of Memphis with her means of inspiration. When she retired in 1950 after 30 years as judge of the Memphis Juvenile Court, she had fulfilled the challenge of being the first woman south of the Mason and Dixon line to be addressed as Judge.

With words as tools, **Elizabeth Meriwether Gilmer** (born in 1870), better known as **Dorothy Dix**, gave such sane and witty advice in her nationally-syndicated and widely quoted columns that she was ranked seventh in a poll of the most powerful women in America. Weaving words into fiction, **Caroline Gordon** received high critical acclaim for her rendering of historical and contemporary scenes. And both as historian and librarian **Mary**

U. **Rothrock** made significant contributions to the state's literary heritage. Her leadership was recognized when she was elected National President of the American Library Association.

In music Tennessee women found a special inspiration and have continued to share a special gift. Their most distinctive voices were found in the highlands in the east, where memories of old ballads still lingered, and along the big river to the west, where laments and blues from another culture reached up from New Orleans. In between was Nashville, where many of the women whose names are household words around the world today initiated their careers.

The great **Bessie Smith**, born in Chattanooga, sang the lyrics of Beale Street's **Alberta Hunter** in the first of her many blues recordings:

> I've got the world in a jug, the stopper's in my hand,
> I've got the world in a jug, the stopper's in my hand,
> I'm going to hold it
> Until you men come under my command."

Winchester's personable **Dinah Shore** and McMinnville's **Dottie West** were home-grown talent. But in Nashville's Grand Ole Opry the **Carter family** of Virginia, Kentucky-born **Loretta Lynn**, and Alabama's **Tammy Wynette** became forever associated with Tennessee.

It was **Kitty Wells**, the most popular female vocalist of her time, who brought a distinctive theme to country music, to Tennessee women, and to every woman who heard her—in roadside honky tonk or elegant parlor. Peter Watrous, discussing Kitty Wells' legacy in *The New York Times* in 1988, pointed out that she was "the first woman to present country music regularly from a woman's point of view. . . . She was marketed as a solo performer, a radical idea in a newly blossoming industry that had previously only experienced women as members of performing families. Her first hit, which went to the top of the country charts, *It Wasn't God Who Made Honky Tonk Angels,* is often credited as the first real woman's song in country music. Within limits, it opened the door for women in country music to express whatever was on their minds."

Zilphia Horton used music for another kind of inspiration. At Highlander Folk School, near Monteagle in the Cumberland Mountains, she collected and composed labor songs from 1935 until her death in 1956. One of her discoveries became a legacy that has reached around the world. Two labor union members from Charleston, South Carolina, brought to Highlander a song that captured the attention of Zilphia Horton and folk singer Pete Seeger, a visitor. They made minor changes in the words and tune and *We Shall Overcome* became the anthem of the civil rights movement.

Here, among the inspired and the inspiring, the courageous and the versatile, is such a one as **Frances Reed Elliott.** In her very heritage of blood she combined the three great strains of early America: Caucasian and African-American and Native American. Her mother, Emma Elliott, was the daughter of a white plantation owner in North Carolina. Her father, Darryl, a sharecropper on the plantation, was the son of a Cherokee father and a black mother. Before their baby was born, Darryl had fled in fear of his life and Emma had been exiled to Tennessee. Here she lived on a monthly allowance from her father, gave birth to the baby she named Frances, and five years later, lonely and tubercular, died.

Little Frances Elliott began a long pilgrimage through a series of foster homes and schools, including Knoxville College where she spent some eight years. Tall, confident, strong and gentle, Fannie found her inspiration in nursing. When she was forced to choose between it and the first man to whom she was engaged, she chose the nursing—and went to the Freedmen's Hospital School of Nursing in Washington, D.C. For the rest of her life—during two World Wars, epidemics, economic disasters—she cared for those who needed help. She was the first African-American nurse to be officially enrolled in the American Red Cross.

When she was still a child herself, Fannie Elliott had declared her dream: "I want to be a nurse and help little children." Her biography has been well-named: *Trailblazer.*

Among Tennessee women, in all their variety, are also the vicious, the bloodthirsty, the destroyers. Such a one was the mother of John A. Murrell, "the great land pirate," whose band of thieves and cutthroats terrorized the region from Kentucky to New Orleans, until he was arrested in 1834. In his own account of his life, Murrell gave credit where credit was due: "I was born in Middle Tennessee. My parents had not much property, but they were intelligent people; and my father was an honest man I expect, and tried to raise me honest, but I think none the better of him for that. My mother was of the pure grit—she learnt me and all her children to steal so soon as we could walk, and would hide for us whenever she could. At ten years old I was not a bad hand."

Here, too, is **Ella** (sometimes Alice) **Pride,** who claimed to be one of the Night Riders when a group of settlers in the Reelfoot Lake region banded together to oppose by extra-legal means the efforts of a land company seeking to control the lake for private profit. Small farmers, hard-pressed sharecroppers and fishermen, invaded by a smattering of riffraff, these "Sons of Joy" and "Knights of Fun," as they sometimes called themselves, were not the type to include women in their revelries and retaliations. However, Mrs. Pride "complained to authorities that she had been stripped and beaten by the Riders until she consented to become their secretary. Forced to wear masculine clothing, she said she accompanied the Riders on their raids under threat of death."

The band finally gave her a whipping for her loose talk. History has concluded that she may have arranged some meetings for the masked band, but it is unlikely that she ever accompanied them.

Night Riders were less discriminating about women as their victims. During the seven months in 1908 when the Reelfoot region was in the grip of terror and violence, women were punished for reasons that bore no relation to the primary purpose for which the band had been formed. One sued her Night Rider husband for divorce, and was brutally whipped with a briar bush. Another was lashed to a tree and beaten because she would not return to a drunken husband.

The predominant image of female mischief and violence that has animated the state's folklore, tall tales and legends, however, has been that of the witch. Sometimes one wonders if the Bell Witch was not for a long time the best known woman in Tennessee, considering the number of stories, reports and books written about this "mysterious spirit. "

In her account, *The Bell Witch of Middle Tennessee*, **Harriet Parks Miller** opened with a merger of mood and fact:

They come when nights are hoarse with wind
And drenched with gusts of rain,
And scratch with pointed fingernails
Against the window pane.

During the early twenties of the past century, a mystery known as The Bell Witch appeared in Robertson County, Tennessee, near what is at present the little town of Adams.

"It was an invisible agency of tangible action, with a voice that spoke at a nerve-racking pitch when displeased, while at other times it sang and talked in low musical tones."

"It seemed bent on tormenting two members of the Bell family, Mr. John Bell and his beautiful daughter, Betsy, hence the name Bell Witch."

In "real life," the witch was identified as one **Kate Batts**, an old lady who seems to have made the fatal mistake of being "enterprising." She was described as "a very eccentric woman." Her husband was incapacitated the greater part of his life and she assumed control of his business. "She was exacting in all her dealings with men and thought everybody was trying to cheat her."

Other women "exacting" in business dealings have sometimes shared Kate's fate of being called witches.

From hidden cabins in fog-shrouded mountain coves to lonely dwellings along the sprawling river bottoms, witches were long a part of daily lore, demanding constant pacification. Tangles in the hair indicated that witches had been riding a person. Twitching of an eye was a sign of being bewitched. Salt sprinkled around a house would frighten witches away. If a knife was placed under the pillow, witches could not harm anyone in bed.

Women as witches were exceeded in folklore only by the number of ways in which women could bring bad luck. When a woman came to the house where a family was moving, it foretold ill, as it did when a woman went into any mine or coal factory or lumberyard. If the first caller on the first day of the year was a woman, bad luck. If it was good luck to start on a journey and meet a man first, just the opposite was true if a woman was the first person encountered.

If superstition endowed woman with supernatural powers, historians and romanticists often placed her on a pedestal of superior graces. Both attitudes removed her from the everyday choices and challenges of the mainstream of life.

The early historian of Middle Tennessee, A.W. Putnam, as he described the women who were family and friends of James Robertson after he moved westward from that first settlement on the Watauga to the site that would be Nashville, invoked the pedestal. He said: "If God made the angels to enjoy their happiness in heaven, he made women to find their happiness in trials, toils, duties, and sufferings on earth, and therefore may they be exalted a little higher than the angels in the world to come."

Would James Robertson's wife, **Charlotte,** have found such homage appropriate? It was she who had helped establish each of those two new communities in the wilderness, she who had borne 11 children along the way, with two sons killed by Indians and one daughter dead at the age of two. And Mr. Putnam tells us that when Robertson would call the Nashville settlement "our promised land," his wife would sometimes add, "The promised land ought to insure rest to its inhabitants."

With James and Charlotte Robertson, with wife and mother, we come full circle in this initial glance at the variety of the Tennessee woman's experience. And we reaffirm that it is these great wives and mothers, so often nameless and forgotten, that we celebrate first in these pages. We remember them not as their husband's possessions but as their partners.

Putnam tells us that many a backwoodsman listed the inventory of his wealth as follows:

The best shooting gun,
The fleetest nag.
The prettiest sister, and
The most fruitful wife.

And he adds, "The wife often had good reason to be jealous of her husband's attachment to the gun and horse."

No it is not the thrust for equality and partnership that dishonors the role of housewife and child-bearer; inequality and the false pride of possessiveness fostered such dishonor. In April, 1977, a press release summarized some of Tennessee's economic sanctions against its women's most fundamental role and contribution, as discovered by a woman's legal group.

"Despite the hallowed rhetoric for the sanctity of home and motherhood," Associated Press reported, "Tennesseans still give Tennessee homemakers a legal back seat." Specific instances: "1. Divorce is usually the only way a wife can enforce support rights, maintenance and child support. 2. A woman can sue for damages for physical injury at the hands of anyone except her own husband. 3. A wife divorced prior to 20 consecutive years of marriage loses all eligibility for her husband's Social Security. 4. The homemaker is not covered by any type of disability insurance. 5. A farm wife who inherits a large tract of land will probably have to pay higher taxes than her husband, although she has co-owned the land and worked it for many years."

Albert Camus, the Nobel Prize-winning French writer, might have been speaking for Tennessee women past and present, red, black and white, when he invited: "Don't walk in front of me, I may not follow. Don't walk behind me, I may not lead. Walk beside me, and just be my friend."

Often that seems to have been the most difficult place for a woman to find and fill.

There was not very much thought given to where the pioneer woman would walk, literally or figuratively. Beside, behind, in front—wherever she walked, ran, plodded, limped, pursued, fetched or carried, the need was for survival, for fulfilling the task at hand.

Sally Ridley Buchanan was one of those pioneers. She weighed more than 200 pounds and she was strong: she could heave a 150-pound sack of corn to her shoulder and carry it, if the need arose. Even more important, she was stout of heart: courageous and kind, winning the respect of all those who lived in the fort known as Buchanan's Station, on Mill Creek in Middle Tennessee.

During the Indian attack on that fort in the autumn of 1792, Sally Buchanan took the place of several men. There were only seventeen men to defend the station against some "four hundred of the flower of the Creek and the Chickamauga," and one historian has said, "There never was such a battle in all the bloody annals of Tennessee."

Perhaps there never was such a defender as Sally Buchanan, either. As the men began to run low on ammunition she "came amidst the raking fire of bullets singing through the picketing" from the painted warriors outside, and with a bottle of whiskey in one hand and an apron filled with bullets she began to distribute her supplies. Again and again she went the rounds.

Harriette Simpson Arnow, who has recorded so splendidly

the history of the Cumberland River country, tells us of another woman in that fort, a young mother: "Half-crazed with fear, a newcomer she must have been, unfamiliar with green scalps and the ways of Indians, grabbed her baby, caught the toddler by one hand, and ran, carrying and dragging children toward the fort gate. She was determined, it was later said, to save the lives of her children by surrendering to the Indians, forgetting in her terror that to open the fort gate by so much as a crack would be the end of them all. She never got to the fort gate. Sally Buchanan ran out and brought her back. . . ."

No wonder that one of the few bronze highway markers across the state which bears a woman's name commemorates "Mrs. Buchanan." Yet there were many who had similar or even more harrowing experiences—capture, torture, even scalpings which they sometimes survived—in their determination to establish homes in a wilderness country.

What is often forgotten is that the pioneer woman was a companion, a total participating citizen in the total life around her, to a degree that would not be evident again until the contemporary thrust toward Camus' ideal. Arnow sees the father's increasing preoccupation with trade, and the centralization of industry away from the family cooperative effort as part of the reason for weakening of the home. "Mother ceased to be a yoke-fellow, becoming instead only another subject moving in a separate and less important orbit, but always fixed around the head of the house, and he in turn orbiting around his occupation, usually business." Arnow concludes that "in general the great importance of the home on the frontier and in the South made the mistress of it a much more important person than is the average woman of today."

Among the pioneers and those who soon followed to build

plantations or cultivate small farms, establish towns and create communities, there were also the African Americans. On John Donelson's flatboat as he and his family came to help found Nashville there were 30 people in bondage. From the mountains, where there were smaller farms and fewer slaves, to Memphis, the center of the state's cotton culture, there were black women who labored in the fields and those who nurtured the young of their own and white families in their formative years. Between them they helped build the agriculture and industry and mould the character of the state.

Sometimes such a one as **Rebecca Budman** might fight for her freedom. She had settled in Smith County in the early 1800's and was known as a free woman. But she lacked papers of proof. It was necessary for her to establish her freedom legally if her children were not to be considered slaves. The county justices let her case drag on, but Rebecca persisted and eventually won the official documents she needed.

Most were not so fortunate. A bloody Civil War would rage across Tennessee before a whole segment of the female population could be emancipated at least legally from forced bondage.

Tennessee's women filled many roles during that war. Whether their sympathies were with the Union or Confederate forces, they took over farms and businesses and carried on husbands' and sons' duties. An example of such partnership was **America Dill's** hegira with her husband, Col. B. F. Dill, and his co-owner of *The Memphis Appeal*, Col. John R. McClanahan, when they had to flee Memphis in 1862. Living when and where they could across the South, carrying their press with them, the Dills wandered until June, 1865, when they returned to Memphis. After her husband's death in January, 1866, until sometime in 1867, America Dill continued to publish *The Memphis Appeal,* at home once more after its long travels.

Enduring the raids and depredations of two armies who were engaged in decisive battles across the state wrought hardship and suffering on the women who were trying to conserve such resources as they could. Worst of all were attacks from the groups who had no loyalties, the "bushwhackers" who seemed to infest every part of the state and prey on those who were defenseless. **Adeline McDowell Deaderick,** who lived on a beautiful farm near Jonesboro, later wrote of numerous visits during the war years from those "bands of marauders." Her experiences were repeated in many other households.

One night, she remembered, "about forty of these men swarmed in upon us like hungry wolves demanding food." They took blankets, horses, food. And later, Adeline Deaderick was stricken when she learned that in at least one case women had become bushwhackers themselves. "The women had become so emboldened," she later recalled, "that they shaved their heads, don'd men's apparel, and entered the pilfering traffic." She said they betrayed themselves to their victims when they began to quarrel over dishes and bed quilts and silk dresses. "'This looking glass is mine, t'other is yourn.'"

In at least two counties, young women organized themselves into unofficial companies to help at the soldiering. Some 27 girls in **Rhea County** raised a cavalry troop in the summer of 1862. Captain **Mary McDonald,** 1st Lt. **Jennie Hoyal,** 2nd Lt. **O.J. Locke,** and **3rd Lt. R. G. Thompson** were elected officers; their chief activity was to visit Confederate companies stationed in the vicinity and supply them with articles of clothing, food, and knick-knacks. They were eventually arrested, transported by a boat known as "Chicken Thief" to Chattanooga, and made to take the oath of allegiance. While waiting for the boat to carry them back home, "they heard that Gen. R. E. Lee had surrendered which was sad news to them."

In the opposite camp were members of the **Blount County** **"Loyal Ladies Home Guard."** When General Sherman came into their county in December, 1863, the six girls of this little band rode out to meet him and tell him that Confederate General Longstreet had quit his siege of nearby Knoxville. They were young and female and their work was unofficial, but under Captain **Cynthia Dunn** the group had been so effective in their efforts that Lt. **Harriett McTeer** was arrested for spying. The husband of **Dora Jackson Birdwell** was killed because he was suspected of spying.

Female spies there were in abundance—from English-born **Annie Law**, tried in Knoxville as a Confederate informer, to Memphis-born **Miss Ginger** and **Miss Lottie**, the **Moon** sisters whose exploits embroiled them in more intrigue than an Alfred Hitchcock movie, and exhibited resourcefulness of spirit and independence of action that left enemies and friends alike in a state of shock and admiration.

Disguised as an Irish washerwoman Lottie carried dispatches from Memphis to Cincinnati, extending her mission at one point even to Canada. Ginny was especially creative. Acting as a bereaved widow, she accompanied a coffin filled with medicine through the Union lines. After the war she raised a black child, an orphan, as her own son, and extended her care to other orphans in Memphis.

In March, 1864, 18-year-old **Belle Edmondson,** who lived on a Shelby County plantation, told of one of her many trips from Memphis as she smuggled goods to Confederate forces out in the countryside. She had to conceal "8 yards of grey cloth for uniforms, 2 large hats, 1 pair of boots, a dozen buttons, cords and tassels and letters." An impromptu headdress was made of the cloth, and she "pin'd the Hats to the inside of my hoops—tied the boots with a strong list, letting them fall directly in front. . . All my letters, brass buttons, money, etc. in my bosom. . . started to walk, impossible that—hailed a hack—rather suspicious of it, afraid of small-pox. . . ." Sometimes whiskey and tobacco were among the supplies this walking (or riding) department store carried in her hoops, bosom, sleeves and head-gear.

Nannie Haskins, in Clarksville, echoed the cry of many a Tennessee woman during the terrible war years, no matter what her political allegiance might be. In March, 1863, she wrote, "once we were a gay and happy family—once there was six of us, now there is three left at home, two have been taken, one is still battling for 'freedom.' Oh God send him back to us, spare him, I pray."

Inadequate hospitals, untrained nurses, and insufficient medical supplies accounted for a dreadful toll of human life away from the battlefield. Tennessee, second only to Virginia in the number of encounters fought across its length and breadth, had need of the women who forged their way into camps and hospitals and cared for the wounded, diseased and dying.

"On whose authority are you acting?" an army surgeon demanded of **Mary Bickerdyke**, who searched out the wounded after the Battle of Fort Donelson.

"On the authority of the Lord God Almighty; have you anything that outranks that?" she responded.

The only woman at the battles of Lookout Mountain and Missionary Ridge, "preparing hot drinks and food and doing all she could for the comfort of the 1700 Union wounded amid the mud and freezing rain," she represented many women in every city and crossroads who came after battles to restore such health and peace as was possible.

There were persons, of course, whose lives had been dedicated to doing away with all slavery, long before it became one of the central issues in that bloody upheaval, the Civil War. One such person was a woman who came from the British Isles, hoping to found in the Tennessee wilderness a totally equal society.

When she was barely seven years old, Frances Wright asked an elderly instructor: "You have told me a great deal about God's son, but you have never told me anything about God's wife."

The little Scot, born in Dundee in 1795, would continue to ask questions and propound ideas to outrage, amuse, intrigue, and stimulate friends and strangers until her death in 1852. Before her third birthday her parents died, "leaving her in possession of a large fortune and an inquiring mind." She used both to promote ideas so advanced that wherever she went she made headlines: advocating economic and political reforms, women's rights, abolition of slavery, universal public education, religious freedom, "and what in today's terminology would he called open marriage and no-fault divorce." Choosing to come to the New World of America rather than to the cultural centers of Europe, she sought to put her ideals of freedom and equality into action.

For her utopia she found a site suggested to her by Andrew Jackson, on the Wolf River, 13 miles from Memphis. Nashoba, after the old Chickasaw word for wolf, she called the farm that covered nearly 2,000 acres. Her primary purpose was to provide a place where slaves could come and work the land, be part of a commune where all would share alike. Eventually—through education and labor that had paid off their purchase price—the slaves would be free and capable of becoming productive citizens, perhaps in Haiti or Mexico, where they could he resettled.

As her vision of Nashoba widened, she sought to establish a community where "affection shall form the only marriage, kind feelings and kind action the only religion, regard for the feelings and liberties of others the only restraint, and union of interests the only bond of peace and security."

Realities of climate and economics, human frailty and perversity, and daily details which could become large problems—these combined with other forces to subvert Frances Wright's purposes. There was, for instance, the fact that from the beginning her plan had been conceived, approved, and directed only by white people. "It took no heed of black people's feelings," one biographer has pointed out. "Blacks could not he expected to cooperate if they had no voice, no vote, no power."

And in one of her earliest letters from her colony, Frances Wright referred to a situation that would remain the thorny problem on this vast farm: "All these small matters (overseeing construction of houses, a water supply, etc.) keep me very busy, for there is nothing more difficult than to make men work in these parts."

The tall, vigorous woman who was such an arresting presence on the public lecture platform or in the drawing room of General Lafayette or Thomas Jefferson, tried to set a good example for her Nashoba neighbors. She labored "like a man," clearing fields of heavy underbrush and stumps, planting an orchard and crops of corn and cotton, until she was struck down by a severe attack of malaria.

From that time forward she was forced to be absent from Nashoba during long periods. Her sister, Camellia, and other members of the colony proved to be poor managers. Their economic situation and relations with the surrounding society became strained to the breaking point. A newspaper editorial said, "Miss Wright has, with ruthless violence, broken loose from the restraints of decorum, which draw a circle round the life of women."

For Nashoba that circle became a noose and its founder was forced to admit, "Collective humanity is alone able to effect what I thought myself equal to attempt alone." In January, 1830, she sailed from New Orleans with the entire black population of Nashoba; 13 adults and 18 children were resettled in Haiti, far from the Tennessee wilderness where they were supposed to be part of a new and better society.

There were many ironies in Frances Wright's turbulent and controversial life; perhaps none was more profound than that involving her child. Frances Wright, a feminist all her life, found one of her irredeemable alienations to be that from her daughter, to whom she bequeathed the Nashoba property.

She died at 57 and was buried in Cincinnati. A New York newspaper published a poem about this woman who had never known "her place."

Oh, Fanny Wright, sweet Fanny Wright
We ne'er shall hear her more,
She's gone to take another freight
To Haiti's happy shore.

For she has gold within her purse,
And brass upon her face;
And talent indescribable,
To give old thought new grace.

And if you want to raise the wind,
Or breed a moral storm
You must have one bold lady-man
To prate about reform.

The experiment in Tennessee, at Nashoba, was doomed but
one of the questions Frances Wright asked would not die: "Fathers and husbands! Do ye not see how, in the mental bondage of
your wives and fair companions, ye yourselves are bound?"

Many other pioneers in many other fields would have to break
lonely trails and occupy solitary citadels before that question
would be seriously raised—or answered.

After the wilderness and its hardships and a war and its toll,
frontiers of many kinds still remained. Education was seen by
many citizens to be the great liberator, yet financial support for
public schools was appropriated in only the most meager sums.
Families scraped together necessary funds to send their sons —
and sometimes their daughters — to private schools. The general
attitude was that public institutions were considered "paupers'
schools."

One versifier summed up the general opinion on what composed an education in Tennessee in 1823, an opinion that persisted for many decades to come. He wrote, in part:

Boys go to school to learn hard names,
To spell, and play at grammar games;
The girls they learn to draw and paint,
Primp up their mouths, speak fine and faint:
This is fashionable learning.

When boys have learn'd that they are made,
To heave the earth with plough and spade;
And girls, that they must toil for man,
Make clothes, wash pots, and frying pan;
They're then prepar'd for learning.

Although **Barbara Blount**, the governor's daughter, and her handful of friends had attended classes at Blount College (later the University of Tennessee) in 1804, making them the nation's first coeds, this practice was soon discontinued. When Mary Sharp College, in Winchester, was opened in 1851, its president's aim was to offer young ladies "the same knowledge, literary, scientific and classical, that has for so many generations been the peculiar and cherished heritage of the other sex . . .or an equality with her brother. . . thus making her what she was designed to be by her Creator, a thinking, reflecting, reasoning being, capable of comparing and judging for herself and depending upon none other for her free unbiased opinions."

By the 1880's there were fifteen women's colleges in Tennessee. As coeducation gradually increased, that number decreased, however. As early as 1867 Maryville College had admitted women, and from the time of its establishment in 1875 Peabody College welcomed women. In 1879 Vanderbilt awarded a diploma to its first female graduate. In the academic year 1892-93 the University of Tennessee began to admit women to its classes. In his commencement address of June, 1894, Judge Edward T. Sanford stated that "the admission of blue eyes and rosy cheeks within the academic halls" was proving successful and "will not detract from their feminine charms nor deprive them of their graces. . . ."

Women were being educated but where were opportunities to make that learning fully useful to themselves and their communities? In 1886 Sarah Childress Polk observed, "It is now considered proper for young ladies, when they leave school, to teach or do something else for themselves. It was not so in my young days. It is beautiful to see how women who go forward independently, supporting themselves in various callings, are respected and admired."

Unfortunately, those teachers received more respect than salary. Their pay was pitifully meager. And Mrs. Polk failed to suggest the "something else" they might do or what their "various callings" could be.

There is no way that all their names can be honored here, names that span time and distance—reaching from **Angie Warren Perkins**, first woman on the state university's faculty, to Memphis educator **Nellie Angel Smith** who earned the first doctorate at Peabody College. Smith insisted that athletes were "good students if they had the time," so she helped them find time as well as incentive for their academic studies. Many of their names will never be known, those who labored in little one-room buildings or later in crowded city facilities, to stimulate minds and offer the rudiments of literacy and knowledge to Tennessee's youth. These women, filling the teacher's role in increasing numbers after the turn of the century and awarded the higher-paying administrator's role much less frequently, deserve our attention and gratitude.

There was one education frontier on which women played a special role: schools for African-American children. Forbidden access to the classroom before the Civil War, blacks were still handicapped after the war by the fact that it was difficult for the Freedmen's Bureau to find teachers for the schools it established. A number of Northern women came to Tennessee to help meet the need.

One example was that of **Emily Austin,** who came to Knoxville from Philadelphia in 1870. As Knoxville's able historian, **Betsey Beeler Creekmore,** tells us, in that same year "Knoxville's first free public schools were opened, in nine residences rented for the purpose throughout the city. Three of the nine schools were for Negro children, and in one of these Miss Emily Austin taught." She raised funds in Philadelphia to help build a more adequate school, and then she raised more money to help establish an industrial training school.

The tablet placed in the school that bears her name says she was "for thirty years a devoted friend of the freedmen, fearless of criticism, shrinking from no duty, unswerving in fidelity, coveting only Divine approval."

Her courage and humanity were akin to that of another teacher, **Margaret Anderson,** who responded to the desegregation violence and crisis in her town of Clinton with rare insight. As guidance counselor to black and white children who were experiencing mob scenes, hate campaigns, and the eventual bombing of their school building in the 1956-57 term, she witnessed both raw evil and unvarnished good at work in the human situation. Some of the girls who would become Tennessee's women of the next generation were memorable: "**Roberta,** whose hunger for learning kept her reading into the night long after the tasks of caring for 11 brothers and sisters were done; **Victoria,** who responded to the white boys' abuse with the tearful words, 'Maybe it will be easier for someone else.' "

In a moving and inspiring book, *The Children of the South,* Margaret Anderson recorded one woman's response to one of the gravest problems of our times. Of her experience in her Tennessee, her South, she concludes, "I have faith that in 'a few more days' home will be a better place. It is a better place right now. By facing our problems on home ground rather than running away from them or transferring them to another section of the country, we not only help the nation as a whole, but we bring stature to the South."

And always there were the African-American women who struggled and attained against incredible odds to make use of every classroom at their disposal. One of the unique stories of American education includes that of the Jubilee Singers, who dedicated their talents and energies to lifting their alma mater, Nashville's Fisk University, out of debt. Consider the story of one of the five women among the nine who made up the original group.

Ella Sheppard was bought out of slavery by her own father; she was smuggled to Cincinnati and given an opportunity to take piano lessons—on condition that she come to her teacher's house late at night and use a back door. Eventually she became the pianist for the Fisk Jubilee Singers as they stirred audiences across America and dazzled royalty across Europe from Queen Victoria to the Czarina of Russia. Ella Sheppard also drilled the individual voices of the singers. From the back door of her timid white music teacher she moved to the entrance hall of palaces and cathedrals.

Pre-school education was the initial challenge that led **Tilda Kempler** to create an organization of self-help community programs in a deeply rural area of East Tennessee's Campbell and Claiborne counties. Third child of a coal miner, Tilda went through the eighth grade, married at nineteen, and finally, at age thirty-two, earned a B. S. degree in elementary education. Then she found that her students needed more than classroom work. She started a pre-school program. That grew into a number of social programs and the formation of the Mountain Communities Child Care and Development Centers (MCCCDC), an umbrella for efforts in job creation, child care, small farming, and other enterprises. It became a model for the surrounding region and foreign countries. A Jefferson Award in 1980, one of the prestigious five chosen from over thirty-three thousand national nominees, assured Tilda Kempler that her struggle *From Roots to Roses,* the title of her autobiography, was worthy of honor.

While numbers of women worked on frontiers of education to liberate the mind, others labored on frontiers of medicine to heal the body. In earliest days, Cherokee women shared with European settlers many of their secrets for curing a variety of ailments. In roots and herbs and flowers of the field pioneer women found useful remedies. They became resourceful in meeting emergencies—from snakebite to frostbite. As midwives they cared for each other during a succession of births that sometimes seemed to come with annual constancy. Families of eight, ten, twelve children were not uncommon on the frontier; John Sevier, one of Tennessee's most revered heroes, had 18 children—two wives.

Combatting epidemics in the cities, as did Memphis' **"Madam Annie"** when she gave her life nursing yellow fever victims in 1818, or traveling into the hill-bound coves of East Tennessee to fight typhoid and diphtheria, as did Knoxville's lovingly-remembered nurse, **Augusta Tamm,** women cared for at least some of the ill and the neglected.

Midwives, nurses, and care-givers to young and old and the afflicted in their homes—yes. But opportunities for women to win medical degrees ranged from limited to non-existent. One pioneer was **Emma Wheeler,** an African American who came from Florida to Meharry Medical College in Nashville where she graduated and married a classmate. The doctors Wheeler entered private practice in Chattanooga in 1905 and by 1914 were able to build

Walden Hospital, the city's only hospital for black patients. Managing the hospital was Dr Emma's special responsibility which continued until 1953 when a public hospital for African Americans was opened in Chattanooga. Emma Wheeler served not a race or a city, but humanity.

When **Henrietta Veltman,** daughter of Dutch immigrants, moved to Paris, Tennessee, from Nebraska, she was determined to have a medical career. At one point she even cut her hair and wore men's clothing while trying to outwit a Kentucky school's ban on women medical students. In 1910, she returned to Paris with a degree from the Chicago School of Medicine, now Loyola University. For fifty years, Dr. Veltman ignored laws and habits of racial segregation, treated anyone who sought her help, and delivered more than 4,000 babies.

To heighten the capabilities of those who would reach out into their communities across their states, and eventually around the world, a Tennessee pioneer in public health took up her work. **Dr. Lucy S. Morgan,** the daughter of **Dr. Harcourt A. Morgan,** well known as president of the University of Tennessee and then as a director of the Tennessee Valley Authority, attended the University of Tennessee, where she taught for a period. After earning degrees from Columbia and Yale universities, she began giving graduate training to public health educators at the University of North Carolina—"a pioneering effort in every sense, for hers was the first such class offered in this country." When the School of Public Health was established at the University in Chapel Hill, North Carolina, she became its first head. Serving the World Health Organization, she eventually gave service to countries around the globe on every continent.

Sometimes the varieties of the world's citizens and their needs, not always medical, reached into Tennessee. One example of the many responses to such needs is found in the **Jewish Service Agency**, and its forerunners, in which Memphis women played a significant role. Before the turn of the century they cared for victims of yellow fever; later they helped meet needs of Eastern European Jewish immigrants, especially those who lived in the neighborhood known as the "Pinch." The newcomers' situation was often poor, "due to low wages, inefficiency, idle seasons in tailoring shops, etc. forcing them to require assistance." Classes of many kinds, a library, clubs for mothers and young people, and a Friendly Visiting Committee were part of the practical response forthcoming in Memphis.

Slowly, women pushed back barriers and entered a variety of professions and occupations. By 1920 history records that Tennessee women "were employed as actresses, architects, artists, sculptors, authors, editors, reporters, chemists, assayers, metallurgists, clergywomen (**Rachel Jones**, probably the first woman resident minister in the state, began preaching in a Friends church in 1868), college presidents and professors, dentists, designers, draftsmen [sic], lawyers, musicians, osteopaths, photographers, physicians and surgeons, teachers, trained nurses, librarians, and as 'unspecified' professional women."

In 1910, a widow, **Mary Treadwell**, and her sister, **Georgia Harry**, both inexperienced in business, established in Memphis the first insurance agency in the United States to be owned and managed by women. Automobile insurance was a new and undeveloped area of the industry at that time and these energetic young women gave it their full attention. Slowly they won bigger business and purchased other Memphis agencies. Grandsons and great-grandsons inherited the success won by two enterprising women.

Another team of women initiated a quite different achievement. The Satsuma Tea Room in Nashville was the idea of **Arlene Ziegler** and **Mabel Ward**. Wandering east and south from South Dakota, where they had taught home economics, they wanted to open a tea room and found Nashville to their liking. Initially they were denied credit by the banks but they opened on a small scale with high standards of quality. Soon they attracted a large and loyal clientele. The success of the Satsuma Tea Room is representative of many such women's enterprises across Tennessee.

By 1920 many women were employed as business executives. **Mrs. Brenda Vineyard Runyon** was an outstanding example of a woman thus engaged. She was a president of the first woman's bank in Tennessee. It was located at Clarksville. It was also the first woman's bank in the U.S.A.

The situation was not as rosy as it might appear, however. One contemporary summary of woman's situation said, "They are filling up the shops and stores, and doing the same work for about half the price that men get, which is a clear gain to the shopkeeper whatever it may be to the home. And they are found in the courts, in the physician's office, on the platform, in the pulpit, on the tripod, everywhere except civil offices, and they are manfully [sic] contending for them. It will be a good day for the old state when women get all their rights."

But there was a little matter of woman suffrage to be resolved. Fundamentally important in its own right, suffrage also became a symbol to women across Tennessee and the nation when the state emerged as a decisive factor in shaping the nation's future.

"Let the women pray and the men vote," Tennessee's governor advised in 1908.

He was giving voice to attitudes and mores that had dominated the national experience since the writing of the Constitution. That document granted the vote to white adult male property owners. The property requirement was gradually abolished by the states, but the race—age—gender requirements remained. Women could share the burden of society but not its most fundamental privilege. Neither Rachel nor Sarah nor Eliza could vote for the husbands who were to become their presidents.

Two other national issues were wedded to the initial thrust for woman suffrage: abolition of slavery and the temperance movement. Women helped work toward these goals also, and the first was achieved in the Civil War. After the war, the Constitution was amended to assure all citizens, regardless of race, color, or previous condition of servitude, the right to vote. Women were still not allowed access to the ballot box.

Susan B. Anthony, arrested and fined in 1872 for voting in New York, became the voice of these silent ones. It was she who wrote the first version of the 19th amendment to the U. S. Constitution, but it would be more than 40 years before the threat of the "petticoat vote" became reality. Such terms reflected attitudes summarized in another male leader's assurance that "the only guaranties [sic] of good government and peace are the ballot-box, the jury-box, the sentry-box, and the cartridge-box — the soldier, the sheriff, the policeman and the gun." Naturally, through time-honored practice, it was assumed that each of these boxes would be held by men.

More gentle, but perhaps even more powerful and pervasive, was the conviction expressed by another political leader on the subject of woman suffrage: "It is far better for society and for the woman herself that woman have her privileges rather than her supposed rights."

Several generations of women had been giving some thought to those privileges and rights, however, and they often found it difficult to determine just what the line of demarcation was between the two. An opponent of woman's right to vote might call suffragists and their supporters "she males," but how did access to the ballot box relate to her femininity any more than her relation to other assorted artifacts of public and private life?

Tennessee suffragists found an answer to this question in a verse that had appeared in a national magazine and they reprinted it for their constituents:

> It doesn't unsex her to toil in a factory
> Minding the looms from the dawn till the night;
> To deal with a schoolful of children refractory
> Doesn't unsex her in anyone's sight;
> Work in a store—where her back aches inhumanly—
> Doesn't unsex her at all, you will note,
> But think how exceedingly rough and unwomanly
> Woman would be if she happened to vote!
> To sweat in a laundry that's torrid and torrider
> Doesn't subtract from her womanly charm;
> And scrubbing the flags in an echoing corridor
> Doesn't unsex her—so where is the harm?
> It doesn't unsex her to nurse us with bravery,
> Loosing death's hand from its grip on the throat;
> But ah! how the voices grow quivery, quivery,
> Wailing: 'Alas, 'twill unsex her to vote !'
> She's feminine still, when she juggles the crockery,

Bringing you blithely the order you give;
Toil in a sweatshop where life is a mockery
Just for the pittance on which she can live—
That doesn't seem to unsex her a particle
'Labor is noble'—so somebody wrote—
But ballots are known as a dangerous article
Woman's unsexed if you give her the vote!

With such responses, suffragists were answering their opponents in kind—with sarcasm and laughter. Certainly laughter had
been one of the most potent weapons used against the group with
which suffrage had early alliance, the Women's Christian Temperance Union. When national W.C.T.U. president **Frances E.
Willard** addressed the group's convention in Nashville in 1887
she called for universal prohibition and the enfranchisement of
women.

A Nashville paper dipped its print in acid to ridicule women
interested in such concerns: "All of the ugly women, henpecked
husbands, chronic dyspeptics and $3-preachers in the state are
urgently requested to meet Sunday night at Crank's Hall, on the
corner of Tincan Alley and Loafer Street, for the purpose of forming a grand central temperance alliance preparatory to the coming prohibition campaign." The coarse satire concluded with an
invitation to hear "Aunt Sooky Fusseel in a profound lecture entitled
'How to Make Water.' Mrs. Sophia Soapsuds, the world-renowned
tongue-lasher, who has scratched three husbands bald headed
and driven each in turn to seek refuge in the grave by means of
strong drink, will read a forty-page essay on 'Red Hair vs. Red
Liquor.' "

The image perpetrated by such mockery was belied by the
women who emerged as leaders of the suffrage cause. Their names

are legion and span the state: **Mrs. T. W. McTeer** in Maryville, who was president in 1898 of the second woman suffrage society formed in Tennessee five years earlier; **Hannah** and **Anna Price** who organized a club in Morristown and "got up a crowd in a hall and had the various pastors of the churches to speak" on equal suffrage in 1900; **Mrs. E. W. Pentacost**, a well known W.C.T.U. worker, and **Miss Eleanor Coonrod**, a lawyer, who became first officers in the Chattanooga suffrage society organized in 1911; **Pauline Townsend** of Ward-Belmont College, who initiated speech classes "to make more effective orators of the suffragists;" **Sarah Barnwell Elliott** of Sewanee; and **Mary Church Terrell** of Memphis, who reminded the state and national suffrage movement gathered in convention that their concerns for justice must be inclusive, not exclusive: "You will never get suffrage," she told the vast audience, "until the sense of justice has been so developed in men that they will give fair play to the colored race. Much has been said about the purchasibility of the negro [sic] vote. They never sold their votes till they found that it made no difference how they cast them. Then, being poor and ignorant and human, they began to sell them, but soon after the Civil War I knew many efforts to tempt them to do so which were not successful. My sisters of the dominant race, stand up not only for the oppressed sex but also for the oppressed race!"

Mary Church Terrell belonged to the aristocracy of black Tennesseans as three dominating personalities of the suffrage movement belonged to leading families of white Tennessee. They were Elizabeth Avery Meriwether, Lizzie Crozier French, and Sue Shelton White.

The dauntless courage of this versatile triumvirate of three-name-ladies created the strongest momentum for that progress summarized in **Mary Ellis Butler**'s description of changing attitudes toward woman suffrage in the city of Jackson: "Hostility in 1913, ridicule in 1914, tolerance in 1915, frank approval in 1916."

Years before any equal suffrage society was formed in Tennessee, **Elizabeth Avery Meriwether** of Memphis published a newspaper in which she advocated votes for women, rented a large theater where she became the first Tennessee woman to lecture for woman suffrage, and presented herself at the ballot box, where she was allowed to vote.

Lizzie Crozier French lived at the opposite end of the state from Elizabeth Meriwether, but they shared the same impeccable family background (important in a region where who you were could often become more important than what you were) and the same indefatigable devotion to their cause.

When an equal suffrage society was formed in Knoxville in 1910, its first president was Mrs. French. The vote and struggle to attain it was only one of this remarkable woman's many concerns, but she understood that the ballot was power. On public platforms, where she swayed audiences with her eloquence, and in private conferences, she argued: "Nobody can revere and respect people who have no power. Reverence and respect are given to people who have power; and by power I do not mean force, but I mean there must be some way to compel."

Mrs. Meriwether had been born in 1824, Mrs. French in 1851, and **Sue Shelton White** in 1887. "Miss Sue" has been described as a "practical idealist" whose "curling brown hair and deep-set brown eyes gave to her countenance an aura of sweetness and gentleness that was belied by the ruthlessness of her aggressive attack in political debate."

Born in Henderson, "her real 'education' began with her appointment as court reporter in 1907." She held this position for ten years in Jackson, the first woman in Tennessee to be a court reporter, and this experience gave her first-hand knowledge of the law and the ways in which it affected women's lives.

Cynics of both sexes had openly hinted and secretly hoped that women's "emotionalism" would eventually lead to a breakdown in their ability to cooperate with each other in attaining their long-sought goal of equal suffrage. When differences did arise, however, in the 1913-1915 period, the result was not what anti-suffragists might have predicted. The rift had grown out of a minor matter—whether a national convention in Tennessee would he held in Nashville or Chattanooga—but what was of major importance was that Tennessee women were not destroyed by differences but strengthened by them.

Professor James P. Louis says: "Rather than fragmenting and demoralizing the women's cause in Tennessee the division created a fierce rivalry between the two groups. This resulted in increased competition for superiority in membership and for 'good works' for the cause. The 'schism' divided the organization but vastly strengthened the suffrage movement in the state."

Sue Shelton White became the most famous nationally of any of Tennessee's suffragists. At the national level she sided with **Alice Paul**'s "militant" approach as opposed to **Carrie Chapman Catt**'s "evolutionary" pace. "Miss Sue" felt that President Woodrow Wilson should he pressured to come out unequivocally in support of woman suffrage. To this end she joined in a demonstration in front of the White House on February 9, 1919, during which she dropped into a fire the "effigy" of the President—a cartoon depicting Wilson making a speech on behalf of democracy with the head of a woman chained to his belt—which a colleague had carried past the police in a folded newspaper. 'Miss Sue' and thirty-nine of her fellow demonstrators were promptly arrested.

She was imprisoned for five days in the old Work House, a gloomy miserable facility which had been condemned seven years before. Then she joined a crosscountry tour in a chartered railroad car, the Prison Special, to 'bring the issue to the people.' "

The issue had been gaining momentum in Tennessee for several years, however. When the 46th annual convention of the National American Woman's Suffrage Association assembled in Nashville in November, 1914, a Nashville paper described the scene in the Ryman Auditorium (which would later become famous as the home of the Grand Ole Opry) as "brilliant" and "inspiring." Yellow, the suffrage color, blazed from elaborate decorations, and the band alternated playing "Dixie" and "America."

The opening welcome by Governor Ben W. Hooper not only set the tone for the rest of the convention's reception in Nashville, it also indicated significant masculine support for woman suffrage. In part, he said, "It is highly appropriate that your progressive movement should unfurl its banners in this, the most progressive state in the South. Our people are not swift in their pursuit of strange doctrines, but they are as a rule open to conviction and tolerant of differences of opinion. Whatever may be our views of the necessity and efficacy of woman suffrage most of us have sense enough to know that it is surely coming in every state in the republic."

The governor's bright young daughter, **Anna B.**, was warmly applauded after her father said, "When suffrage comes to the women of Tennessee I shall derive one substantial pleasure from it, if I am still living. That will come from the joy and exultation of my little daughter, who has been a positive, pronounced and persistent suffragist since she was 9 years old."

The growing success of the woman suffrage movement was demonstrated most clearly, perhaps, in the fact that in 1916 the first organized opposition appeared in Tennessee. A chapter of the National Association Opposed to Woman Suffrage was organized in Nashville. Its most outstanding leader was Miss Josephine Pearson, of Monteagle. By 1920 Miss Pearson was president of the Tennessee division of the **Southern Woman's League** for the Rejection of the Susan B. Anthony Amendment.

As a "Daughter of the South" she rejected the suffrage struggle "for strong-minded women and weak minded men." Appeals went out to citizens and legislators to reject the Federal Suffrage Amendment. One such appeal warned: "It carries with it more than white woman's suffrage. Lurking in it are three deadly principles:

1st. Surrender of state sovereignty.

2nd. Negro woman suffrage.

3rd. Race equality."

When **Mary Church Terrell,** of Memphis, joined with others attending the National Association of Colored Women's Clubs convention at Tuskegee Institute, Alabama, in July, 1920, in recommending that "colored women give their close attention to the study of civics, to the laws of parliamentary usage, and to the current political questions, both local and national, in order to fit themselves for the exercise of the franchise," such advice was seen by the Southern Women's Rejection League as introducing a new Reconstruction—only this time the carpetbaggers would be female.

Race, the Bible, and henpecked husbands were all invoked in opposition to woman suffrage.

"I am not fighting you," a genteel doctor in Nashville assured the suffragists, "I am only trying to save you from yourselves." He then went on to describe some of the participants he had observed at a suffrage convention. "There seemed to be a large contingent of the Connecticut spinster type—prim, nice and exact, thor-

The summer weather in Tennessee was hot and some of the tempers were even hotter. Bands played, cartoonists flourished, orators waxed eloquent, and the women wearing their yellow ribbons—signifying determination to win the vote—marched along the streets of Nashville. Such public display confirmed the pessimists' warnings about the demoralization of the family and society if women should be allowed the right to vote.

oughly at home in any presence. . . school teachers and govern-esses. . . .

"Next came a rugged brand, strong and aggressive, from the West and Northwest, the region whence sprang this latter-day abomination of split skirts, breeches, top-boots, cross saddles and straddle-riders. . ."

"Finally, there was a small contingent of typical Southern women, that I will liken to a bevy of white doves—symbolic of peace, gentleness and love—lamely and feebly attempting to fol-low and to imitate the eagles and other kindred birds of less degree in their magnificent aerial sweeps and predatory swoops. They were, of course, highly decorative. . . ."

By the summer of 1920, when Tennessee legislators made ready to vote on the proposed Nineteenth Amendment, the lines were clearly drawn. Miss Pearson and fellow anti-suffragists stated in a widely-circulated petition: "Because it is our fathers, brothers, husbands, and sons who represent us at the ballot box (we oppose suffrage). Our fathers and our brothers love us; our husbands are our choice, and our sons are what we make them. We are content that they represent us in the corn-field, on the battle-field and at the ballot box, as we represent them in the school room, at the fireside, and at the cradle. . . ."

Nashville's **Mrs. Bettie M. Donelson**, a long-time leader in both the suffrage and W.C.T.U. movements, replied to such an argument: "Since I discovered I possessed a thinker, I have preferred to be recognized as a citizen, instead of being classed with the 'unpardoned' criminals, lunatics and idiots. The highest law says 'taxation without representation is tyranny,' and this was the outgrowth of that little tea party many years ago. So I ask, are the daughters of 'men' made of different material from the sons of women?"

Thirty-six states were needed for ratification of the Nineteenth Amendment. By summer, 1920, 35 states had ratified, eight had rejected, and there was no time for another state, except Tennessee, to act. The right of American women to vote in the approaching November election depended on Tennessee. Governor A. H. Roberts called the legislature into special session and announced his strong support for ratification. Each side marshalled forces for a closely contested vote.

Mary French Caldwell, a young Knoxville reporter, covered that special legislative session for her paper—and remembered 50 years later what this event in Tennessee women's history was like. "It was a 'wet' August, just wet enough to make the vegetation greener than usual, and to set fields and fence-rows ablaze with the gold of the official suffrage colors. Black-eyed Susans and other yellow wild flowers, and, toward the latter part of the month, the golden-rod, bloomed in profusion.

"Everyone favoring woman suffrage wore either a yellow flower or yellow ribbon—and Nashville gardeners did not hesitate to strip their gardens for flowers to decorate suffrage headquarters and place in the lapels of loyal legislators and new converts to the cause."

Mrs. Carrie Chapman Catt, who had come down from New York for this pivotal vote, did not remember the scene so pleasantly. She had not been encouraged by local suffragists to participate too heavily in activities; during the weeks of deadlock and discussion and unbroken heat, she sat in her stifling hotel room and waited. On August 15 she wrote, "I've been here a month. It is hot, muggy, nasty, and this last battle is desperate. Even if we win, we who have been here will never remember it with anything but a shudder."

Mrs. Catt and all the others did not have long to wait. The Senate voted for ratification but the House was locked in a tie vote. "Both Sides Gathered Here For 'Verdun' Battle," newspaper headlines proclaimed.

And no two women waited more eagerly for the result of breaking that tie than Catherine Kenny of Nashville and Abby Crawford Milton of Chattanooga. These two forceful, far-sighted leaders had invested time, toil, and political talent in liberating women from second-class citizenship. Catherine Kenny combined intellectual brilliance with a political sense for organization. Abby Milton, wife of a well-known newspaper publisher, George Fort Milton, held a law degree but never practiced in Tennessee. Equal suffrage was the cause that took her across the state and kept her in Nashville that long hot summer, participating in what many considered "the fiercest legislative battle that ever was waged on this continent."

As yellow roses and red roses flooded hotel lobbies, restaurants, and legislative corridors, proclaiming their wearers' approval or denial of woman suffrage, the decision for the nation hung by one vote. If the amendment failed now it would be another generation before the opportunity for women's equality at the ballot box would come again.

Then a curious thing happened: Harry T. Burn of McMinn County, who had voted with the antiratificationists on an amendment issue, voted for ratification when the resolution was brought to the floor.

Harry Burn's vote, which had won equal voting rights for 17,000,000 women, was due to a woman's influence. **Mrs. J. L. Burn,** "a widowed landowner without representation," had been reading the newspapers in her home in Niota but she had not found any reference to her son, Harry, and his stand on ratification. She wrote him a letter:

> Dear Son: Hurrah and vote for suffrage! Don't keep them in doubt. I notice some of the speeches against. They were bitter. I have been watching to see how you stood but have not noticed anything. Don't forget to be a good boy and help Mrs. Catt put 'rat' in ratification.
> Your Mother

That letter was in Harry Burn's pocket and on Harry Burn's mind when he cast his decisive "Aye" for ratification.

One of the women standing just back of the rail that separated legislators from spectators during that vote was **Anne Dallas Dudley**, who had been president of the first Nashville Equal Suffrage League in 1911, and was its president in 1914 during the convention that she felt marked the turning point in the state's suffrage struggle.

Anne Dallas Dudley brought a necessary ingredient to the long hard battle for the equal vote: her social distinction. As others contributed their special talents or resources to the cause they believed in, so—without ever having it bluntly stated—Anne Dallas Dudley lent the stability and prestige of her name and family to woman suffrage. She also lavished time, effort, and money on the work. Her speeches were effective; one address to a labor group won front-page newspaper coverage and several thousand converts—and "she went home and cried all night at the sight of her name in headlines."

A classic picture of Mrs. Dudley with her two small children serenely gazing at a picture book was widely used with some of her forceful letters, statements, and articles on suffrage. "Much of the success of the cause," one reporter could write, "is attributed to her charming personality, unusual beauty and characteristic graciousness." She didn't fit the suffragist stereotype that the anti-suffragists had been constructing for so long. But then she knew the danger of stereotypes.

She could come from the luxury of a gracious home and plentiful means to help wage battle for a spacious dream. "We have had a vision," she said in 1916, "a vision of a time when a woman's home will be the whole wide world, her children all those whose feet are bare and her sisters all who need a helping hand; a vision of a new knighthood, a new chivalry, when men will not only fight for women but for the rights of women." And, in an article to a Nashville newspaper, Mrs. Dudley wrote: "There is one great essential for belief in the advancement of women, and that is, the belief in women themselves."

Her efforts and those of the other stout-hearted hundreds of practical visionaries who worked for woman suffrage helped women believe in themselves. It was—it is—a belief, a faith that needs constant reaffirmation.

Euphoria over the successful ratification vote soon faded under the harsh light of political realities. The women began a disillusioning discovery of what politics could or could not accomplish and what citizens, for that matter, would or would not do. Tradition, apathy, timidity, and outright opposition conspired in various measure to halt the women's rush to the ballot box and participation in Tennessee's rough and tumble process that often accompanied Tennessee politics. Predictions were optimistic following that victory in August, 1920: "In another five years half the legislature (or Congress) will be female." Hardly. More than 70 years later their numbers could be counted on the fingers of a woman's hands.

"Sue White," one historian has said, "wanted more than partial-suffrage, more than suffrage itself. What she wanted was the legal equality of women with men. What she sought was the opportunity for a woman such as herself to take up a man's tools and compete on equal economic and political, as well as social, terms in a man's world. Unlike many of the more idealistically-minded suffragists, she did not seek to remake or 'purify' the man's world into a feminist image."

Some of the supporters and opponents of suffrage saw the results of thoughts such as Sue White entertained. One of the women stated: " 'Equal pay for equal work' is my war cry. . . . I am tired of seeing women do the work of big, strapping, able-bodied men, and then receive a delicate, frail, emaciated, feminine wage for it. . . . It is my humble opinion that political power would set this matter right."

On the other side, a doctor diagnosed dire consequences for women who entered the marketplace: "The woman who spends the whole day at a desk, in the law courts, or in a house of assembly, may be a most honorable and most useful individual, but she is no longer a woman, she cannot be a wife, she cannot be a mother."

Practical politician Ed Crump of Memphis, who had overtly supported woman suffrage as it gained momentum toward victory, privately wrote to a colleague that extension of the poll tax to cover women would substantially help control their vote.

Ironically, abolition of the poll tax was one of the early causes taken up by the Tennessee branch of one of the strongest women's groups that grew out of the suffrage movement, the League of Women Voters. Before suffrage, a struggling League was formed in Tennessee with **Abby Milton** as its first president. She was seeking to promote a spirit she affirmed when the Nineteenth Amendment was ratified: "I had rather have had a share in the battle for woman suffrage than any other world event." She said the thrill of victory was like "that our ancestors had at the Declaration of Independence." But in this initial effort, the League did not flourish.

When a stronger League was organized October 15, 1936, in Knoxville, it became the sixth in the South to be recognized by the national group. "Among the first issues tackled—and which took years to see accomplished—was abolishing the poll tax as a prerequisite to voting. To make its point on that issue, Leaguers would have 'poll tax dinners.'"

An early example of the dynamic personality, professional talent and organizational ability which would characterize many of the leaders of the Tennessee League of Women Voters was **Dorothy Stafford**, who served for three terms, 1938-1940, as Knoxville's president. Besides abolition of the poll tax, the drive for improvement of the merit system in state government, more efficient state and local programs for public health, permanent voter registration, and strengthened child welfare laws were on her agenda. Among those women who gave Dorothy Stafford special support in those early years were an "outsider," **Opal David**, wife of a young T.V.A. administrator who had just moved to Knoxville with that powerful regional innovation, and an "insider," **Lida W. Ross**, the League's first president and member of an old Tennessee family.

Mrs. Ross represented those best of Tennessee's women who were willing to assume leadership in their community. "More than any person I've ever known," Dorothy Stafford later said, "Mrs. Ross; had the capacity to listen, her mind ever open and receptive to new ideas. With a deep sense of social justice, in situation after situation she stood firm in the face of challenge."

It was **Molly Todd**, a dynamic adopted Tennessean who revived the Nashville chapter of the League of Women Voters in the early 1940's and became its president in 1948. A campaign to register voters was followed by support for a Tennessee Constitutional Convention where Molly Todd was a delegate. She was in the lead organizing women for support of consolidating city and county governments. Nashville became the first city in the United States to adopt Metropolitan government. Her leadership at state and national levels has addressed such continuing challenges as tax reform, civil rights, the environment — in short, the issues of a viable democracy.

The League of Women Voters became one of the earliest voices discussing the issue of a state income tax. Neither advocating nor opposing such a bill, the League followed its purpose of introducing issues that merited thoughtful public attention. An income tax remains high on the agenda for Tennessee debate.

Involvement in the League of Women Voters first stirred Louisville native Jane Eskind, to political participation. "I thought if you wanted to change the way things were, you may have to change the people doing them," she said. And she became the first woman in Tennessee to win a statewide political election.

Even as she labored most devotedly in the vineyards, Tennessee woman was slow to receive leadership roles at the highest levels of organized religion. Rural church or stately cathedral or urban temple, or any gathering place where those seeking spiritual guidance and nourishment might congregate, found a goodly part of its support among its women. They have brought their money and their talents into the fold. And in founding hospitals and hospices and schools, creating havens for the neglected and rejected on the fringes of society, they have ministered to the human family.

One particular group of professional women have been especially representative of both an Old and a New Tennessee. The newspaperwomen and novelists, vigorous individualists have made history even as they recorded it.

Across the state, most of the early female journalists had entered magazine journalism or newspaper publication after the deaths of their husbands. In Nashville, **Rebecca Bradford** continued issuing *The Nashville Examiner* after her husband's death in 1814. In Memphis *The Southern Homestead*'s literary editor was

L. Virginia French during the 1850's. *The Harriman Record* had women printers before 1900.

Forerunner of all of these was **Elizabeth Roulstone.** On November 5, 1791, her husband, George Roulstone, of Rogersville, began publication of the first newspaper in the Tennessee country. When the paper moved to its neighboring city it became *The Knoxville Gazette*, and after Roulstone's death his widow continued its publication. In 1806 she was also elected Public Printer "to print the laws and the journals" of that body, and thus she became the first woman in Tennessee to be elected to a public office by joint vote of the General Assembly.

It is also significant to note that after Elizabeth Roulstone remarried, William Moore moved the printing plant to Carthage. A widow's property became the property of her new husband. Even though she died at the early age of 51, Elizabeth outlived her second husband. Her son, James Roulstone, had taken over publication and editing of the newspaper. In a long and loving tribute to his mother at her death he paid her the highest compliment he knew: "Her mental powers were strong and masculine—her persevering spirit unconquerable—no difficulties could appall her—no occurrence could rob her of that energy and decision which so strongly marked her character."

James's condescending (and socially acceptable) description of "strong" mental powers that were an asset normal to only one gender reflected a myopia influencing the struggle of women who wished to enter the world of journalism.

When **Will Allen Dromgoole** was born in 1860 in Murfreesboro, her unusual name may have foretold a woman of "persevering spirit." She had an interest in writing which her mother encouraged, while her father promoted her interest in law. However, Tennessee did not allow women to practice law in the state. Will

Allen was elected twice to serve as a clerk in the state senate, but then she turned to journalism. A series of well-received magazine articles was followed by a job on *The Nashville Banner* where she became a regular columnist. When World War I erupted she enlisted as a warrant officer in the U. S. Navy. Her columns provided readers with personal wartime encounters that expanded their horizons. Later she continued to share discovery of her own locale until her death in 1934.

They were courageous and versatile—**Pattie Boyd,** who has been called the "first woman's page editor who was a woman" at *The Knoxville Journal;* and **Zella Armstrong,** of Chattanooga, who owned and published a weekly, *The Lookout;* and **Lucy Curtis Templeton,** whose 57 years at *The Knoxville News-Sentinel* included being the first woman telegraph editor in the South, book page editor, and a revered columnist. "Miss Pattie" and "Miss Zella" were sometime arbiters of the society about which they wrote; they knew not only their own genealogy but that of most of their friends. But Lucy Templeton would not accept being called "Miss Lucy." She considered it "sissy."

Sissies they were not, these pioneers in domains that were peculiarly masculine. It has been said that when Miss Pattie first asked for a place on her newspaper as a society writer, she was told that there were no women on the staff. "I know there aren't," she replied, "and that's why I want to begin the work."

When Lucy Templeton first went to *The Sentinel* offices in 1904 to learn to be a proofreader, she was the only woman who had ever been on the second floor of the newspaper building. "The printers immediately resented the feminine invasion," an associate later wrote, "but she soon won their respect and affection. By the time her birthday came, they gave her an umbrella and lauded her in a speech."

EDITH O'KEEFE SUSONG

Edith O'Keefe Susong's portrait hangs beside those of many distinguished colleagues in the Journalism Hall of Fame at the University of Tennessee. Even more important to her would be the family continuity at her newspaper, through her daughter and son-in-law, John M. Jones III, publisher of *The Greenville Sun*. Both the co-publisher and editor are her grandsons, the Lifestyle editor is a granddaughter-in-law, while a grandson-in-law is Vice-President of the Media Services Group owned by the family: eight newspapers, two specialty newspapers, and four radio stations. Another grandson was awarded the Pulitzer Prize for a *New York Times* article, and her daughter, Arne, continues to write the weekly column Mrs. Susong made the most popular feature in the *Sun*.

Photo courtesy of the University of Tennessee.

Whether or not anyone ever gave **Edith O'Keefe Susong** or **Nellie Kenyon** or **Ruth Sulzberger Holmberg** an umbrella, they have been lauded for their contributions to Tennessee. In her excellent study, *Selected Women In Tennessee Newspaper Journalism*, **June N. Adamson** has said of Mrs. Susong that she began her long career as publisher of *The Greeneville Sun* in 1916: "The setting was the conservative upper East Tennessee town of Greeneville. Mrs. Susong had one strike against her, being a woman. She also had a second. She was a divorced woman with two children to support. That she was able to hold her head high, go about her work, take the divorce as a fact of life but never as a stigma in such a time and place, is almost as remarkable as is her contribution to journalism and her region."

"Miss Edith's" head was always high, as were her personal ideals and her public goals for her community. Beginning with a $4,000 mortgage and an "utterly and completely antediluvian" plant, her part of the divorce "settlement," she entered the newspaper world. Many times a man would come in to renew his subscription of one dollar a year. "He would give me an icy stare," Mrs. Susong later recalled, "look around and say, 'Hey Sister, where's your Pap?' When Pap did not show up to take the money he would not entrust it to a female. I was subjected many times to the painful experience of seeing that dollar I needed so badly walk out of my office." She was frank in her later assessment of her position as a woman in a man's profession: "I always found being a woman a handicap in the newspaper business."

It was a handicap she overcame. After she had been in publishing for more than 50 years, the secretary of the Tennessee Press Association said of her, "There is no more distinguished person in Tennessee, and her paper has had a long and distinguished history."

Influential politically, she also became a moving force in the industrial development and agricultural improvement of Greene County. She helped her area diversify from a one-industry, single-crop county. Promoting the best of the new, she also helped preserve the finest of the old: traditional values of family (her son-in-law succeeded her as publisher and her grandson became editor of her paper), service to community, and one of the historic homes of the state.

As a reporter for *The Chattanooga News* from 1925 until 1940, and for *The Tennessean* in Nashville after 1940, Nellie Kenyon learned her profession well. "Listen—that's the main thing. Know the subject, and ask questions."

She listened and asked and wrote outstanding articles about the Scopes Trial in Dayton, when Clarence Darrow and William Jennings Bryan debated the theory of evolution; about President Warren Harding and later President Franklin D. Roosevelt from personal interviews; about Al Capone on his way to prison and James Hoffa, ex-president of the Teamsters Union, during his trials. Petite (barely five feet tall), flamboyant, persistent, she faced the problem common to women in business and professions everywhere. "I was never discriminated against as a woman except in salary," she once noted. Then she recounted the confrontation which occurred when she learned that one of her male colleagues was paid more than she was. The managing editor reassured her that she was as good a reporter as any man on the staff. "Then I asked why I wasn't paid the same. The next week I got a raise."

Ruth Sulzberger Golden Holmberg was not born in Tennessee, but when she returned to Chattanooga to live, it was, indeed, a return. Her grandfather, Adolph S. Ochs, owned *The Chattanooga Times* before he developed the present *New York Times*. Her brother became publisher of the New York paper and Ruth Holmberg publisher of the Chattanooga paper. Described as "the brilliant one" of her distinguished family, her contributions to her paper's and her city's development stressed educational and cultural affairs. Under her leadership the church page, financial page and woman's page received fresh treatment.

At a time when the South was undergoing tumultuous change and meeting some of those changes with violence, this woman publisher reaffirmed her confidence in the state and region. "I'm excited about this part of the world," she told an interviewer. "I think we've shaken a few things out of the magnolias. Newspapers have to provide leadership."

From **Elizabeth Roulstone**'s pioneering effort to the present, no Tennessee woman has had a greater influence on American letters than **Viola Roseboro.** Her largely unknown career can serve as a bridge between the women journalists and the women novelists of the state's history.

Viola Roseboro, born in Pulaski on December 3, 1857, has been called a "kind of feminine Dr. Johnson without his touch of pomposity and without a Mrs. Boswell." It is unfortunate that there was no Mrs. Boswell, for V. R., as she was sometimes called, was—in the best and strongest meaning of the word—a character, unique and paradoxical. Generous in her passion for discovering talent and encouraging its development, she was also frank, suspicious of organizations and "respectability." Perhaps it was partly due to her upbringing as a Southern lady that she felt confined in her candor. A friend said that V. R. once "remarked that the greatest defect of modern civilization was the absence of any place where one could adequately insult people. Either you were in the relationship of guest and hostess or you were both guests of someone else, and when you chanced upon each other at the Grand Central Station, there was no time for you were dashing for a train."

Viola's grandmother was a niece of **"Bonnie Kate" Sherrill Sevier,** and the girl grew up with a strong sense of frontier history and the lives of frontier women. From public "readings" while she was still a child, V.R. went on to the stage, an embarrassment to her preacher father and teacher mother. When she finally moved to New York City, she became a free lance writer and eventually a manuscript reader for the S. S. McClure publications. In the latter role she exerted a power that was important and little known to the general public.

Her biographer, **Jane Kirkland Graham,** has written: "It was through V. R.'s intuition about good writing when she saw it, that Mr. McClure acquired the reputation of knowing a good story from the other kind. Soon after *McClure's Magazine* began publication, V. R. became its permanent Manuscript Reader; through this work her influence on a generation of fiction writers came about as naturally as falling rain. She was the core of the magazine, often unknown to its new editors. . . ."

Impressive—"she had a habit of authority"—compared to George Sand in appearance, half blind, and often ill, she discovered or encouraged a list of writers whose names include O. Henry, Jack London, Booth Tarkington, Willa Cather, and Wilbur Daniel Steele—and she won a circle of friends wide enough to include poet Rupert Hughes and politico Madam Frances Perkins, U.S. Secretary of Labor.

Viola Roseboro died in 1945. In her 87th year she directed that a treasure she owned, a counterpane "spun, woven, and embroidered in the home of John Sevier on Nollychucky Creek," by her grandmother under supervision of Bonnie Kate Sevier, should be sent to the "Historical Museum of Tennessee."

By such slender yet tenacious threads are frontiers past and modern interwoven. If few know her name today or acknowledge the role Viola Roseboro played in shaping America's literary taste, many know the names of those she served as mentor, friend, and catalyst.

Playing a role quite different from that of any other woman journalist in Tennessee but sharing with each of these others a keen intellect and determination was **Ida B. Wells.** Through the paper of which she was co-owner and editor, the *Memphis Free*

IDA B. WELLS

In 1878, Ida B. Wells parents died in a yellow fever epidemic. At nine years old she began to learn ways to be resourceful.

As a young woman, she believed that when she purchased a first-class train ticket she should have a first-class seat. She was forced to leave the train. Ida B. Wells believed that murder by lynching should not have to go unchallenged. She was forced to leave Tennessee. But Ida B. Wells never left her convictions. Eventually it was not she who changed, but the South and the nation.

Courtesy of the Department of Special Collections, University of Chicago Library.

Speech and Headlight, she battled one of the greatest evils of her own or any time: lynching.

Born in Mississippi in 1869, educated there and at Fisk University in Nashville, she became a schoolteacher in Memphis, and invested the money she saved from teaching in the newspaper where she refused to work until she was given a position equal to that of the two men who were its proprietors. Then she used its pages to combat the rising tide of white racism that was moving across the South, the state, and the city. One evidence of this lay in the statistics of lynching, averaging more than a hundred a year during the 1880's and 1890's. The horrible practice reached its peak in 1892, with 161 recorded lynchings of black men and women.

Three young Memphis black men were among that number, and 23-year-old Ida B. Wells came to their defense. The three victims had been arrested as a result of friction growing out of the establishment of a grocery store financed by some of Memphis' most prominent black elite. Economic competition and unfounded rumors combined to create an atmosphere in which nine white men dragged the young blacks from the Memphis jail and took them to a vacant lot near the railroad tracks where they were shot.

Thousands of black Memphians turned out for the funeral procession, while hundreds (perhaps as many as 2,000) fled the city in fear and despair. Ida B. Wells voiced their rage in her editorial demands that the murderers be brought to justice. "We ask this in the name of God and in the name of the law we have always obeyed and upheld and intend to uphold and obey in the future." She supported the black community's boycott of city streetcars. She denounced the threadbare excuse for many lynchings—alleged rape of white women.

A mob broke into the newspaper offices, destroyed its printing presses and made a bonfire of remaining copies of the paper. Only hours before, friends had spirited the fiery editor out of the city; enraged white citizens threatened to lynch her if she returned.

Ida B. Wells did not return. As historian David M. Tucker has written, "After 1892 she alone launched the crusade against lynching in the South which gained the nation's attention." She also spoke before international audiences—often holding Memphis up to shame in her description of atrocities she had recorded there. When lynching was finally stamped out, Ida B. Wells' anger and courage could be accorded part of the credit. Attractive, dauntless, careful to base the evidence used in her editorials on white documentation, she was a free spirit demanding for black Memphians, black Tennesseans, black Americans "what decency and equality of law had always demanded."

Nikki Giovanni never edited a newspaper but in her volumes of poems and her autobiographical statements in prose she bears spiritual kinship to Ida B. Wells. In the book, *Gemini,* and numerous poems she has given us harsh, affectionate, intimate glimpses of what it was like to grow up black and pretty and talented in her native Knoxville. It has been said that she relates in a special way with older women and with adolescents. "To love her is to love contradictions and conflict," a friend wrote. Perhaps it was ever thus with creative spirits, especially those who had to come to terms with the special circumstances of being female.

Those circumstances may help account for the fact that several of Tennessee's women authors have produced but a single volume on which their reputation is established. Spanning the state and the century for examples, there is **Frances Boyd Calhoun** in Covington and **Mildred Haun** in Hamblen County, East Tennessee. The former's story of a 6-year-old boy who goes to live with a maiden aunt in a small Tennessee town, *Miss Minerva and William Green Hill,* was published in 1909. Readers across America responded to it warmly—through 50 printings and eventually a series, written after Miss Calhoun's death.

Mildred Haun's *The Hawk's Done Gone* received no such popular reception, but through the years since publication in 1940 it has gathered critical acclaim and special devotees. Perhaps no novel written in Tennessee has ever depicted the life of its women in more cruel and stoical terms. Mildred Haun herself was a shy, reticent woman who died in 1966 at the age of 55. Her only book grew out of studies of mountain folklore and ballads that she had written for her M. A. degree from Vanderbilt. All of her stories are narrated by women, industrious and enduring, whose dignity is destroyed repeatedly by the indolence and almost casual brutality of the men ruling their lives. Yet her stories are not propaganda tracts; they are rich with humor tempering tragedy, with human frailties beset by supernatural forces.

The variety of life depicted by Tennessee's women seems boundless.

Early in 1868, the editor of *Godey's Lady's Book*, one of the nation's leading magazines, sent an inquiry to an unknown writer living near Knoxville, Tennessee, who had submitted a manuscript.

"Sir, Your story. . . is so distinctly English that our reader is not sure of its having been written by an American. We see that the name given us for the address is not that of the writer. Will you kindly inform us if the story is original?"

The "Sir" was a woman—**Frances Hodgson**—who had thought it best to assume a masculine name (and the local schoolmaster's address) as she tested her talent for writing. She informed the editor that she was English and had been only a short time in America. In June, *Godey's* published her first story and at 18 Frances Hodgson was launched on the career that would make her one of the best-loved writers of successive generations of readers discovering her classics, *Little Lord Fauntleroy* and *The Secret Garden*. After her marriage to Dr. Swan Burnett, of New Market, she acquired the surname that would become famous around the world.

The years spent in Tennessee, just after the Civil War, were formative ones. Although she eventually moved from Tennessee, in later stories and novels **Frances Hodgson Burnett** returned again and again to the rural scene and characters which were part of her earliest experience of America.

Her writing brought her fame on both sides of the Atlantic,

along with the misunderstanding and stereotyping that afflicted other, less successful, women writers and artists. A small example was the nickname "Fluffy," derived from the fringe of hair she fluffed up to conceal a prominent forehead that would have been considered "noble" for a man. Her son observed that the nickname "was a betrayal of her real character." Certainly it did not suggest the hard labor that made this woman cry out on occasion against being "a pen-driving machine."

Sometimes she was praised, sometimes criticized, for being the "New Woman." Her successful career, her eventual divorce, the sheer energy of her drive and forceful personality, made her a candidate for the title that was sometimes derogatory, as in a couplet:

New men, new manners,
New women, no manners.

Mrs. Burnett, although she was first and foremost a storyteller par excellence, was also thorough in her depiction of locale and of the social conditions surrounding her characters. One of her early stories, *Seth*, is set in a Tennessee mining village called Black Creek. It is peopled with immigrants from Lancashire, England, who have come to work in the mines, and their condition— this is in the 1870's—is not glossed over in any way. The pivotal fact of the plot is that the young miner, Seth, is not a young man but a girl seeking to work by any means available. As in many of Frances Hodgson Burnett's books, a number of realistic themes are introduced here in a popular, seemingly effortless, fiction.

Another Tennessee woman, a native this time, won a large audience during the latter decades of the 19th century and the first decades of the 20th century. **Mary Noailles Murfree** was attuned to the social nuances and overt hostilities of her time, however, and she assumed the name Charles Egbert Craddock. If her writing failed, she did not want the stigma attached to her family (the town where she lived, Murfreesboro, was named for her ancestors), but more important, she knew that writing was not considered a proper field for a woman to enter. She also suspected that she would receive more respectful editorial attention if she used a man's pseudonym.

In May, 1878, the *Atlantic Monthly* published her first short story. Editor William Dean Howells was delighted with the response and continued to publish the stories of M. N. Murfree, as the author signed her name in letters to him. When Thomas Bailey Aldrich succeeded Howells as editor he was even more enthusiastic about this writer who depicted the lives and folkways of Tennessee mountain people with the combination of realism, romanticism, and rich dialect that became known as "local color" writing. Her 25 novels established her as a master of this school of fiction.

One of the small bombshells of literary history erupted when Mary Murfree walked into editor Aldrich's office in Boston on March 3, 1885, and announced that she was M.N. Murfree— Charles Egbert Craddock. Aldrich had difficulty recovering his composure, as did guests at a dinner party he had arranged for that evening, where William Dean Howells and Oliver Wendell Holmes and other notables discovered that the guest of honor was "a Tennessee lady." The hostess was so disconcerted by the unexpected sex of her guest that she addressed Mary Murfree at the dinner table as "Miss Craddock."

Such a situation would have amused **Maria Thompson Daviess,** whose chief activities led her to be designated "suffragist and author." Her home was at Sweetbriar Farm, near Madison. Her reputation as a novelist was nationwide, for popular stories with titles such as *Rose of Old Harpeth*, *Over Paradise Ridge*, and *The Road to Providence*. But in two other works of fiction, *Equal Franchise* and *The Elected Mother*, she depicted women struggling to integrate themselves into the mainstream of life.

The *Elected Mother* opens with its central character, Mrs. Pettibone, returning from a visit to Wahoo City where she has encountered women's clubs and the cause of woman suffrage for the first time. She informs an astonished neighbor: "Yes, I'm thinking of beginning all over with Pa. I've been married to him forty-three years next November, and I'm afraid it will go kinder hard with him, but he will have to be led easy and blind-like to the fact that woman's day has dawned. She's been down trodden, geared up uneven, stalled up in a house over a cook stove, poked fun at by love-making and things of that kind until she is such a poor weak creature she is in danger of just going on permitting it and being happy in spite of it."

Later, Mrs. Pettibone describes her experience of "the high vault to the woman side of the fence," as she visited with one of the feminist leaders: "We'd first talk safety-pins and crocheted socks and then about the dreadful sweat-shops and what they do to women. Then we'd veer from short petticoats to the property laws what let a woman work her life out helping her husband buy a farm and then at his death be sold out of it on account of having only a dower interest. We'd plan a little silk coat and end up with a prayer for the noble women teachers that a he-school board makes work longer hours than any little whippersnapper college

boy that's teaching for a stepping-stone, and for much less pay."
What was said sounded to Mrs. Pettibone "like a psalm of life
written in Revelation style."

Other Tennessee women writers have depicted experiences
drawn from living in some distinctive part of the state. **Evelyn
Scott,** in her *Background In Tennessee*, published in 1931, found
her hometown of Clarksville both fascinating and frustrating. She
longed for kindred spirits with aesthetic yearnings and standards,
and remembered one woman with special clarity: "The most
literarily-inclined professional of the people among whom I grew
up was **Mrs. Elizabeth Meriwether Gilmer,** who gave me my first
birthday party, and was later known as **Dorothy Dix.** She was
plump, brisk, quizzical, dictatorial, and engagingly animated;
kind, too, I believe, and eminently practical and sensible."

Across the state from Evelyn Scott, the mountains found two
interpreters in **Laura Thornborough,** whose *The Great Smoky
Mountains* was published in 1931, with its special emphasis on
the many trails and byways its author had hiked, and **Elizabeth
Skaggs Bowman,** whose *Land of High Horizons*, published in
1938, combined history and personal accounts of some of the hill
people its author had known.

Along the way from Burnett and Craddock to **Anita Clay
Kornfeld's** *In a Bluebird's Eye* (1975), and **Lisa Alther's** *Kinflicks*
(1976), Tennessee and America were shaken by social changes
that erupted with a force and consequence equal in many ways to
that wrought by the atom bomb. Kornfeld's novel, tenderly evok-
ing the depression days during which an 11-year old girl grew up
in the coal mining country of Tennessee, combines qualities of
both yesterday and today in its narrative and revelations. Alther's
story, especially that part depicting a girl's high school experi-

ences in the fictitious town of Hullsport, in East Tennessee, during the 1960's, is hilarious and raunchy. For its antecedents we might have to go all the way back to some of those American writers known as Southwest humorists—one of the greatest of whom was Knoxvillian George Washington Harris, with his swaggering, irreverent, shocking character, Sut Lovingood. Lisa Alther's non-heroine, Ginny Babcock, shares, in a more sophisticated setting, many of the old frontiersman's howls and belly-laughs.

Two writers especially representative of the variety of Tennessee woman's experience are non-native **Joyce Carol Thomas** and native **Florence Cope Bush**. In fiction and drama Thomas, an adopted Tennessean now a professor at the University of Tennessee, has brought the black experience to compelling life. Bush has given her East Tennessee mother a warm reality in her non-fiction *Dorie: Woman of the Mountains*. A National Book Award to Joyce Carol Thomas and a Tennessee History Book Award to Florence Cope Bush verify the uniqueness and universality of women's stories in our literature.

What a varied lot they are, these Tennesseans and their interpreters—the few mentioned here only suggesting the whole broad range of the numbers who have defied prejudices, overcome circumstances, and helped us understand ourselves and each other more completely.

It wasn't easy, being a woman on that early frontier—whether you were a Native American woman fleeing from your village during a raid by white pioneers, or a white woman defending your lonely cabin in a wilderness outpost, or an African American woman tending cook-pots or cotton fields or children, all belonging to someone else.

It wasn't easy, being a woman on a later frontier—that faced by **Emma Bell Miles,** for instance. Physically fragile from the day of her birth in 1879 until her death not quite 40 years later in Chattanooga, this wife, mother, writer, painter, teacher, journalist was a passionate participant in the world around her.

It was a dual world. One part consisted of the art school in St. Louis where friends sent her to develop a natural talent, and the cultured and privileged world of Chattanoogans who gave her commissions for paintings and journalistic writing jobs when she desperately needed economic help. The other environment on Walden's Ridge was that of the mountain family into which she married, a "life sentence at hard labor," she once wrote, with miscarriages and five children—one dying, half grown, of scarlet fever. Frank Miles' health was also poor, work on the Ridge was irregular, and he was impractical about money.

Emma Bell's perception led her to admire and share this mountain man's sincerity and to identify with his homespun family and community way of life. Her practical needs drove her to paint and write and publish and sell wherever she could, in leading national magazines or among friends in the city. Her book, *Our Southern Birds*, illustrated with paintings she completed during her final bout with tuberculosis, was published after her death. Her book, *The Spirit of the Mountains*, remains one of the first and one of the few balanced and compelling portraits of Appalachian people and their values. But when *The Spirit of the Mountains* was published in 1905, it received not a single review that can be discovered today.

As quietly, as wastefully, as its author left her world, this landmark work of Southern literary realism and original insight and interpretation slipped into oblivion. It was republished in 1975; its portrayal of some of the gentle young mountain girls and

WILMA RUDOLPH

High school teammates called her "Skeeter."

After her Olympic victories the French newspapers called her *La Gazella Nera*, "The Black Gazelle." To the Africans she was "The Black Pearl." And the Russians crowned her "The Queen of the Olympics."

She returned home a celebrity—and said, "What I like about being back in Clarksville, everybody here just treats me as 'Skeeter,' and I feel so at ease here. Now that I'm back, I feel that Tennessee is just the place for me.'

Photo courtesy of Coach Ed Temple.

enduring old she-eagles of the hills, and its revelation of her own yearning, divided, inspired spirit, adds new dimension to the courage and the variety of Tennessee women's history.

It wasn't easy then, it isn't easy now, being a woman on many frontiers.

Nothing has been easy for **Wilma Rudolph.** She was the twentieth of 22 children. Her mother worked as a domestic and her father was a railroad handyman. As a child she suffered pneumonia, scarlet fever, and polio and wore a brace on her leg when she was six years old. It was not an auspicious beginning for an Olympic medal winner but her mother's determined effort to take her

PAT HEAD SUMMITT

All-Southeastern Conference forward, Lisa Harrison, a senior on Summitt's 1993
team, speaks for many: "I cannot say enough about what she means to me and what
she has done for me as a person and a player. She is really a great coach."
Photo courtesy of the Nashville *Tennesseean*.

to Meharry Medical College in Nashville for weekly treatment
continued until she could walk. Encouragement of track coach Ed
Temple inspired her to run. To run in America, in Australia, and
in the 1960 Rome Olympic games where she won three gold
medals, broke two world records, and brought the crowd to its
feet in waves of applause. When she joined the Women's Sports
Hall of Fame in 1980 she became the first black woman to receive
that honor and the first to so honor the Hall of Fame.

Again, on the frontiers of athletics it hasn't been easy to be **Pat
Head Summitt.** Growing up in Montgomery County she played
basketball with three older brothers and discovered, in junior
high school, that her county had no girl's basketball team. Her

DOLLY PARTON

Used with permission.

She has been described as sassy, flashy Dolly Parton, the leading lady of country music, a pop-rock megastar, but Dolly has never minimized her flashiness or denied her mountain heritage. In the September 16, 1974, *New York Times*, reporter John Rockwell wrote, "She is an impressive artist. Her visual trademark is not far from that of Diamond Lil: A mountainous, curlicued, bleached-blonde wig . . . and outfits that accentuate her quite astonishing hour-glass figure. But Miss Parton is no artificial dumb blonde. Her thin little soprano and girlish way of talking suggest something childlike, but one quickly realizes both that it is genuine and that she is a striking talent."

Possessing one of the valiant features of Tennessee woman at her best, Dolly can laugh at herself, as she did when she told a Las Vegas audience, "You'd be amazed how expensive it is to make this wig look this cheap." It is this "infinite variety" of Dolly, her blending of make-believe and reality, that is a trademark of her impressive success. She has said it best, "I think one big part of whatever appeal I possess is the fact that I look totally one way and that I am totally another. I look artificial, but I'm not."

family obliged her talent and yearning and moved to neighboring Cheatham County. In high school and at the University of Tennessee Martin she played basketball and after receiving her Master's degree at the University of Tennessee Knoxville she became the women's coach there in 1973. Her record is impressive: three national championships, an Olympic silver medal, and recognition as national coach of the year. When she became assistant athletic director at the university and was offered a five-year contract she won another first for Tennessee woman.

Equally important to Pat Head Summitt's success is her recognition as a role model for those women on her team. Demanding respect, she instills self-respect. Discipline is a large part of the learning on the court or in the classroom. Among those who stay

SARAH CANNON, 'MINNIE PEARL'

"Minnie Pearl is never sick, never discouraged, never in a bad humor—she is always smiling, always entertaining," Sarah Cannon says of the character she created and who now "belongs to the world."

Sarah Cannon's private courage in undergoing surgery for cancer in both breasts has been sustained in part by Minnie Pearl's gift of laughter. "Laughter," Sarah Cannon says, is "God's hand on the shoulder of the troubled person."

Photograph used with permission, courtesy of the Grand Ole Opry.

with her program for the full four years, 100% graduate. She speaks proudly of that record.

Frontiers of entertainment do not yield easily, even to the talent of West Tennessee-born **Mignon Dunn** or East Tennessean **Mary Costa** of Grand Opera renown, or **Dolly Parton** and **Minnie Pearl** of Grand Ole Opry legend. Or whether you are one of the young producers, script-writers, scene designers, or actresses moving from Tennessee to the national entertainment scene. But Dolly Parton's little coat of many colors, many scraps, and Minnie Pearl's straw hat with the dangling price tag, remind us that songs and laughter are a common bond around the world, and women of courage can overcome many challenges early or late in life.

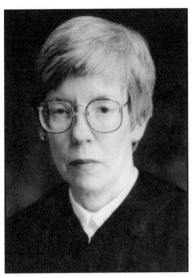

Photo © Harry Butler, used with permission.

MARTHA CRAIG DAUGHTREY

Breaking barriers that limited women in the practice of law became a habit for scholar, teacher, prosecutor, and judge, Martha Craig Daughtrey.

Perhaps her sense of democracy was especially appropriate when she participated during April, 1991, in an American Bar Association-sponsored delegation to Romania to consult with the drafters of the new Romanian constitution.

Judge Daughtrey was member of a council far distant in time and place from the one where Nancy Ward's uncle, Cherokee leader Attakullakulla, had asked, more than two centuries earlier, where the women were in councils with the white Americans.

Frontiers of law are becoming opportunities.

The first woman on the faculty of the Vanderbilt School of Law and the first woman to serve as an associate justice on the Tennessee Supreme Court, appointed in 1990, was **Martha Craig Daughtrey** of Nashville. And in 1993 President Clinton appointed her to become a federal judge on the Sixth Circuit Court of Appeals.

One newspaper editor observed, "As far as records tell and anyone can remember, Daughtrey has been the first woman to hold most of those posts [prior to the federal judgeship]. She may have been a first, but no one can accuse her of being a token. She has a reputation for hard work both on and off the bench. In addition to her work in the justice system, she actively promoted opportunities for women and minorities in the profession and has given much time to improving legal education."

Thus, opening one frontier leads to other challenges.

It isn't easy to be on national, on world frontiers.

Pauline LaFon Gore knew frontiers were not easy from the time she entered the Vanderbilt University School of Law in the early 1930's and found only three other women enrolled there. Before she received her degree she had worked as a waitress at a hotel near the state capitol and met a fellow law student and school superintendent named Albert Gore. In 1937, after both had graduated from law school, they were married. Although Albert was the one who eventually became a distinguished United States Senator, there was never any doubt that Pauline's intelligence in legal and political matters and her common sense instincts in human relations made her a full partner in their success.

Their example may have helped **Mary Elizabeth Aitcheson** (better known as Tipper) **Gore** confront a more recent frontier with her husband, Albert, Jr. as he became Congressman, Senator, and Vice-President of the United States. With a Master's degree in psychology Tipper has not settled for easy roles of leadership. Violence on television, children's issues (she and the Vice-President have four children) and mental health are among the debates she has joined with courage and well-disciplined vigor.

Perhaps Pauline and Tipper Gore experience something in common with Tennessee's three wives of United States presidents in earlier generations. It is necessary to know and to appreciate how strong the bonds were between the members of each of those couples. Rachel and Andrew Jackson, Sarah and James Polk, Eliza and Andrew Johnson, walking together into history as Camus suggested. With Pauline and Tipper their places have been similar, neither following nor leading but beside their Alberts, on a new frontier.

That new frontier beckons not only Tennessee woman in her own place but women around the world. Disease, poverty, discrimination, ancient hatreds and new violence in any place threatens the social fabric everywhere. And research repeatedly reveals that around the world women, not men, are most often the breadwinners — growing, harvesting, processing the food. But even as they sustain life they earn less, own less land, and suffer greater poverty in old age, while bias against women is cited as the single most important cause of the continuing population explosion.

Tennessee woman is akin to all these women.

I met her recently standing in a schoolroom door. Her face was shining with hope and shadowed by uncertainty. "So another year begins," she said. "We have to make it work." I waited as the smile disappeared and was replaced by a firmness that must have been on the faces of generations of Tennessee women before her. "We will," she promised.

Here she is then, Tennessee woman, as richly varied as the natural world around her —
    wearing linsey-woolsey and sable, breaking paths through the wilderness and outer space, birthing babies and plowing fields and accepting the toast of kings.

Here she is —
scolding and singing, stirring apple butter in a copper kettle
and stirring the voiceless to action in her own behalf.
Proud and humble, fascinating in a hundred different ways,
she has persevered—and sometimes prevailed. Her challenge is
not past, her story is not finished. This part of her history is just
a beginning, an invitation for you to go and discover Tennessee
woman for yourself—and help write her future, our future.

The End

Index

About the Author

Wilma Dykeman is the author of 16 books of history, fiction, biography, social commentary, and travel. Three of these were written with her husband, James Stokely, and one with each of her sons, Dykeman and James Stokely III. Her articles have appeared in most of the nation's leading magazines and she is a regular columnist for the editorial page of the Knoxville, Tennessee, *News Sentinel.*

She has served on numerous women's commissions and on the boards of educational and financial institutions, often as the first woman participant. She holds two honorary doctoral degrees.

Awards include a Guggenheim Fellowship, a Senior Fellowship of the National Endowment for the Humanities, the Governor's Award for Contribution to the Humanities at the Southern Festival of Books, the North Carolina Gold Medal for Contribution to American Letters, the Thomas Wolfe Trophy, and the Hillman Award for the Best Book Published in the U.S. on World Peace, Race Relations, or Civil Liberties.

Honored by historical and environmental societies she has served as Tennessee State Historian since 1982 and is a professor of English at the University of Tennessee.

Lectures on a wide variety of subjects permit her to enjoy her favorite hobby (and sometimes profession) of travel. Visits on five continents have strengthened her awareness of the uniqueness and universality that co-exists in our lives.